GOD-SPEED

Jorge Luis/KITO
GOD-SPEED

Published by BooxAi
ISBN:978-965-578-463-3

GOD-SPEED

TRUE STORY OF EXTRATERRESTRIALS AND MILITARY BEHIND IT

JORGE LUIS/KITO

CONTENTS

CAUTION   vii

Chapter I   1
"Use me God"!

Chapter II   10
That which controlled Us, Perfecto Mundo

Chapter III   17
"Sperm Eaters"

Chapter IV   24
Who is the eater of time and money?

Chapter V   29
"I want a new Body, can you help"?!

CHAPTER VI   36
"What is your name?"
What he saw.

Chapter VII   46
"Rules Of Thumb"

Chapter VIII   50
"What Does It Eat"

Chapter IX   64
"THE RICH AND NEEDY"

Chapter X   74
"LISTEN TO ME, WITH ALL DUE RESPECT!"

Chapter XI   93
Danger Money

Chapter XII   102
"GOD OF PITY"

Chapter XIII   111
"Kairos"

Chapter XIV   120
"Mythical Cursed Gold!"

Chapter XV   133
"FRIENDS FROM SPACE"..

Chapter XVI   144
"Its The Elephant"!

Chapter XVII   158
"Pig-Mentation"

Chapter XVIII   172
"Secret Knowledge"

CAUTION

**DECEPTION, SATELLITES, COLDWAR,
MONSTERS IN A LAB, ABSORBING EVEN OUR
PRAYERS IN THE NIGHT WITH
COMPUTERS AND EYES PIERCING OUR HOMES**

Cigarette
- A thin cylinder of finely cut tobacco rolled in paper for smoking.

To the ones we've loved, admired,
and carried. When It gets dark and nothings

there remember the music we made and shared. I love you, my life.

Thanks for the trust and letting little things get by that stung so violent run

from cursing.

Thank you to those who made us think.

CHAPTER 1
"USE ME GOD"!

The Year 2018 Greensboro NC

Nueva Vida, Had a walk through heavens fruits of knowledge commencing meditation finding peace with spirit ever so brilliant echoed this plane of existence. God's location still at large, what created this? One young man asked for so long. Coming from a religious background like others, regardless of Christian origin or Muslim text. To the promise of glory and triumph in this venture of the day. A gift of life was it "God ever so merciful" who truly watches our growth?

Grabbed by the hand led to church as a child because your mother brought you, or as a grown man, it's a spiritual search for the need of mental to heart enlightenment parallel to the creator. Had the day for a quiet young man beat up from life's excuses give him the need to call on "Deities" Contemplating. Regardless of this attempt for such connection of inner stabilization, one must have patience.

To better understand such circumstances in fulfillment. Its as you are told, what you listen to. Yet must not go one ear pushed out thee other. From the gospels to the song, although what does the preacher tell. A wise lesson or a portion of his life and bible. Skipping the introduction of baptism, does a story ever shock you? If not, you might even be in the right place although at the wrong time. A walk of faith where everything really just works, although we give thanks to God for what the time did for you.

In prayer some ask for forgiveness or a blessing, being personal or for someone else in hopes it heal. Biblical notes spoke lore of hero's, who with such divinity, aided in understatement and wise perception to move the people. "Use me God" they'd speak to such figure in the dark, next to a bed or near a throne. They died with such belief. The rightful cause to do so in class is marking history. Accidental or by miraculous luck, that story or thee story is a Miracle. Given the rarity of uncommon results.

"I CALL TO YOU MY GOD, IN EFFORTS TO COMMUNICATE WITH YOU DIRECTLY. THERE SEEMS TO BE SOMETHING WRONG WITH THE AIR, I ASK YOU TO GIFT ME WITH THE WISDOM OF SOLOMON AND STRENGTH TO GROW AS A MAN. I COME TO YOU AS A FRIEND AND ASK FOR MENTORSHIP. I WANT TO HEAL THE NATIONS AND USE MY VOICE FOR GOOD. USE ME GOD, I HAVE WHAT IT TAKES. FATHER I HOPE EVERYTHING IS WELL" ,"I ASK FOR A CHALLENGE"

Such a miracle for a man to pray and call to his CREATOR in this formula of instant life. Such a unique prayer to ask this Wise Shadow to "Use him", himself given up as a host. In hopes of washing the world of sin with courage as his ancestors. To use your voice and to walk as a strongman. The Date of such event isn't highly ever noted although I have one for you. <u>September of 2018</u> and the uniqueness of such practice is that God Answered right back. Just not the one we were accustomed to understanding, nor being brought up to learn of.

This god showing itself. By it was "IT". Like a deformed Valkyrie, with all due respect, "IT" was short of structure and with Stout physical qualities revealing as a creature! Having been "IT"s true face not of a man in a beard and robe. But yes a happening of the third kind in the most random of locations the young man quickly thinks in a controlled state of mind.

Noting sometime after more details as followed.

Drooling, backing away and grinning with large black oval eyes as the background itself. With a skin complexion of Grey and white. Damn thing was smiling. It didn't exactly form sinister, more miraculous was how docile it presented itself.

Staring back from within the consciousness of prayer, a deep meditated state host at awe.

Had "IT" with its pale skin come closer in a form of flattered appeal of an expression. Would the luck of a young pioneer not realize what the summons would bring forth. Yet nothing was said, Lasting only a few seconds following the quiet and eerie introduction not long after disappearing from his sight. With both eyes now wide open and his mouth dropped to the floor with the biggest grin of disbelief and self achievement. Rare of what happened in a room pondering.

In such intervention the host who called upon God, Invoke instead this impostor. Didn't flinch but beckoned to it while their eyes still closed shut. Intrigued and dazed that such a being showed itself in mental connectivity to answer thous prayer. "Hey!.., hows it going??" The dimwit host calls to it with unusual surprise. "It" doesn't say a word just lingering off slowly back to the shadow and disappears from sight. Eyes open up and disbelieved that such proportions of something to reveal in a unique manner, compelled and interested to show itself for a fraction of time.. Is this still a miracle of the capture of a rarity?, Only thing in mind. Prayer Ends.

With all but thanks to the same God, one was calling for in the case that maybe this was the answer. From the darkness rose the extraordinary. Slender malnourished. To the modern age this was Alien. Extraterrestrial of origin for nothing like on Earth could match such physical character.

Humanoid of appearance, two eyes one nose with a small mouth yet *drooling and grinning* without speaking a word as if it shared excitement as the young host. Day was coming to night, for it has been an hour since the meeting with the Grey friend. Leaving the host confused, dazed, hungry to see more of his new friend "IT".

The next day, a restart this time prepared. All around the same time span an hour before sundown. There must be continuation to such spiritual research and its answer. One would be foolish without question, clumsy to not try again.

Naive or intelligent to do so it was worth another attempt. A do over in efforts to seek another chance at summoning his "fallen angel". So once again, next to a bed and on his knees the host commences.

"Thank you, I come humbly in approach to better understand the circumstance in hopes Lord Father to answer once again. Forgive me for asking..did God send you?"

At first. Nothing would seem out of the ordinary. No flaws to the instants from the previous night's prayer. No tampering with vision while eyes remained closed as most, if not all personal prayers would adjust to. That is how we, if not most of all speak to the creator. Lashes folded down and our voices heard personally from within one are such spoken words told.

It couldn't have been an invitation, yet who did the host at this point try enticing to appear? Jesus's Father or was it "IT". Foreign tooth fairy of the shadows here to collect a man's final baby denture. Results were there just the other night, Took a moment again in prayer, he got what he searched for.

All details of such was as humble as it could be. *"Use me God", "I wish to wash the Earth with healing waters, a voice to aid the people".*

Then the *magic happened..* like a fish on the line it hooked on to something, rare but the prayer worked you could say. A sound that connected to the host had echoed in, a voice. Simple yet artificially rythmmed as if it were programmed to be versatile and directly treating the guy as if he we're being looked for. Loud and accustomed being linked towards the independent good boy of a listener. It spoke as it followed.

"There he is!" The voice coming from outside the patio which was across a sliding glass door in front of the bed where the sacred kneeing took place. Opening the door, up a white cloud, sounding as if a conversation ran along then the laughter of a young couple, chattering from above. Had the sky been alive, then a male voice followed as if of similar age of the host. In toned like two birds in a pot. Spoke in Modest-English *"MY SON IS COMING HOME"* as if UN- meaningful and sarcastic. Chuckling. To which in then the voice of the male, along with its too hidden companion following both break of invisible presence.

This communication of "voice" was enough to claim it as a second or third intruder had made efforts of mental telepathy. Modern man,

What was present was technology in the middle of some kind to communicate and check him-out. Telekinetic one would accept as. Technology of course present yet unfamiliar to our human ingenuity, the real question is now. Is this malicious? Although nothing was present in the skies that would otherwise show itself. Regardless of the identity of the host who started the prayer was agnostic, in Reality yet wishful to speak to thee Divine God of Solomon and Moses, Muhammad and his prophets. Someone or something answered.

This was not the biblical figure one would've been keen to hear about. It seemed as if a doppelganger or at wishful understanding this was the closest approach God was able to connect with. Maybe even the start of a labor he'd have the boy perform. The scenario of such in contrast was very displaced and non entertaining for whatever the case. It stretched the reason to comprehend what is normal and why it seems so flawed. As far as what comes in turn of how people or humans operate. This example was not at all simple to grasp. FOR *IT* DOES, WAS NOT, what we are accustomed to.

Cicadas heard from the trees, night came to be. The boy slept in peace and nothing could raise him to such trepidation as to what happened there in his apartment following such entry after prayer. Dream came to be, Falling and diving unto a cool dark ocean above from a cliff, the atmosphere before him alien and ambient of stars. Water crashing as he makes splash. The vision of what was ;follows him to hear a woman's voice speaking in English;... "When we got here, all we found were old buildings." He sees the bottom of such ocean and it was too dark with a light pushing out the distance, submarine exotic craft of sorts slithering the floor.

High beams that stretched to scavenge and rapidly check the underwater future city flooded that once was. It moves so quickly like the rhythm of a line in the game of worm. Moving accurately left and then right, dodging pillars the height of mountains. This object is like a chain of orbs connected to one another traveling smoothly and swiftly.

Host wakes in drift to find two strange and uneasy characters in his room. As if a couple in hologram projection takes shape in front of him.

One was of the women that spoke aloud, Being raised in a Pentecostal Christian formed foundation. Remembering, the young man thought, Had it been the same female deity mentioned in biblical texts. Where Great King Solomon for example, Changing his view of Almighty God and betraying his own senses right after. In this case it was big and had to be important in this episode of echelon dwellers. Same mortal asking for wisdom. Enticed by another deity, claiming itself even besting God of the Israelite's. Yet this being wasn't claiming higher power but of equal.

Her image having frame of a robotic , body figure was like heavy and widen. Yet she acted as if mannered of interests. There was a second figure more eye catching and Rarer of form then anything any other demon the bible could conjure. A large creature with a small black box as face, similar of appearance to a maggot. Of it remained observant as the robotic female. Both contained in their own portrait. As if unique to each of their style and taste. You couldn't tell if either were smiling, there were only a few words from the robotic which did all the talking in this nightly horror episode. "We are here to congratulate you creator"!, in an artificial feminine voice. Boy dropping his sight for a second a quick faint, winks. Only to find them both vanished, absent and gone from sight, quick as they first came to his room.

It got darker, the night was yet to creep with what was next. So exhausted from the wreck of watch. It didn't take long for a faint back to bed. Raising his head again randomly looking around his room, suddenly eyes wide open! A pale skinny extraterrestrial satyr of sorts! Walking with his legs bent back like a grasshopper its body slim. No sign of openings or other forms usual of the human body. Roams closer to the host. It was Grey with a shade of blue and it had no mouth the kid couldn't scream. So petrifying to watch how advanced and simple of a design the specter being shaped. "Hello Creator".

By the time it had reached near closer to his arm, the boy had no ability to move his body nor scream. While in shock, the alien figure started evaporating going invisible and gone.. chuckling. 'What the fuck was that..!" boy passes out.

Completely drained. Rest of the end of that night. It was unforgettable, without a doubt impressively gross.

It is to be taken noted that these events are of rarity, authentic as the day. How often it happens with other people remains a shroud of reality, most things are barely documented. Although this is the story of a young man who raised in the American cool breeze State of North Carolina, described these events very up until recent of 2018 following up to now. This is what many would consider to lounge and indulge into as fresh as the sour enters, tasted with. Watch the Gucci, This is what's real.

***Cigarette*, A True Story and Study of Space Rulers and Monsters.**

Perhaps I should smoke one. I caution not to.

CHAPTER 11
THAT WHICH CONTROLLED US, PERFECTO MUNDO

"If I told you an Elephant tells me jokes would you believe me?"

Then there was fire, Mortality's element . Weeks went by an the answers seems uncontrolled from the heavens, insanity as if the optimism of an individual left broken. "There was no reason to be in this place", For the mind could not handle such. Manic. Days went with riddles and no actual answers for what was real in a young man's new predicament. This soon to be unholy situation, DAMN, DAMN, DAMN.

There was voices in the head, calling from many spectrum's of what was UN-normal since the first happenings. No sight of what was once there. For several days, yet there was what appeared to be some sort of blessing from an alternate being claiming lord's place. What followed was of an Epic, the formula of religion at last an answer, what to do with it.

God, the Divine Creator. Deity of the Israelite's. Voice towards Moses and Abraham spoke. Wise, Sane, Loving Real as you'd expect it. At a defense one would listen yet be ready for attack. It left the host in tears and tremble. Even allow oneself to continue listening at such and gave in at servitude "God, what can I do for you?" One would follow at a major glance.

A voice spoke in such matter it came consciously and when no one else seemed to be there. Not when a servant is most vulnerable but when Host and this Spirit is both Available. Same night, Coming as a second following up of visitations from beings at prayers point. A fragrance de bouis of "IT" the moment an amateur scholar would hope for.

Voice of such instance that followed was of God. Thee God!

Out of madness rose Creator.., spoke in perfect English and Spanish. Impressive catch, Damn voice is as hard to capture as you might think. Everything had to be perfect to lure a deity in your home.

Harnessing it, the time of present. A Trillion bucks to that of Like Big Game.

"Vas aser lo todo en mi palabra," (You will do all in my word)
"Usa tu vos", (Use your voice)
"Ay insectos donde quiera." (There are insects everywhere)
"Te lo doy todo" (I give you everything)
"Perfecto Mundo", (Perfection of World) *"Magnificent." "Don't let me be the last one."*

Said in words that sounded to heighten both valor, and strength. This is rare of. Such in matter that left any vulnerable to succumb that yes to confirm it is.'"IT". In all respect what one would have figured to be the true voice of how "Divine hence speak amongst". There was no image but a placement fixed in the mind to believe that at front could be of portion of what God Is.

Chills running still.

For instance, without the need of hallucinogenics. One would see figures that would tamper with normal functions of a brains neuron mechanisms pattern. Where the eyes seem focused, a mirage and picture on the ground and carpet. Still leaving mesmerized thoughts of how it was being done. Shifting perception of reality.

This would seem very useful to the smart man to believe its use of some kind of military like procedure. Confusing, debilitating, water boarding tactics. For this was not normal. Images that placed together in front face were not of the sane of heart. Could be used as diversion or representation. Regardless this spiritual search of "Father understanding" would have to cease and come to an end.

It was an overall and clear assumption to me that the experience towards the host at early stages would have been. What was modest investigation that it had to be several causes to such. Maybes left a door open, perhaps indeed technological.

There was a formula to over look the hosts and evaluate.

Tests of the Minds well being, Body's physical state in the case of any recent injury, thee spirit another as part of the trio- effort to see of any changes to a normal attribute. For one it would be a physiological tamper of himself as male to have gone through trauma of sorts. No irrational behavior yet did seem resemblance to schizophrenia.

With all due respect however even our medical and best science could only give doctored primitive medicinal and comforting clinical aid to their examples. For what we are taught, Even personal evaluation didn't occur to have any proof of physical temperament to show that there could have been work related, or pain from a nerve cracking or brain injury to any recent cause for the continuation.

Then there was the spirit, a man's prayer is told to be heard, also took notice of. Many recent leaders of faith have spoken in preaching of such communication and interests giving testament and example. Allowing the mass to know and wonder the miracle of Religious Creator speaking to them as a means to send a message.

Useful, to believe that a man called upon and saw something else. How would others taken notice of such story? In this generation many things are present including evil ones. A look of someone or something called on Merciful and saw a being at its place. Sure there were prophets in the past although not all man are, known of or have taken the journey to be walked in the realm of our plane as one. This was different, this was alien.

In the world of extraterrestrial and open mind this was in fact a Grey, matching descriptions and its lore of traits. Large Oval eyes, Silver skin tone from what the name derives. Yet it came in front of a man's head near sundown. In a suburban area in a American south eastern state.

Although this was not of what was expected to be the guardian of faith nor the face of superior. At first glance this could not be the expectations nor could it match in personality of what multiple entities first entered, including as the dancing lure of two. A guy and a girl hidden in a cloud. Not one of these scenarios were of relation to what he saw. As-well, as heard recorded before from the get go.

Days went on, so did the change in weather. Human enlightenment was involved in the young man's journey to understand what was to adjust, testing all of what he could hold and balance. Was he still a Host? Pride was present, had thee involvement that what tampered with him. Beyond that momentum of interference from his normality. There was a tense manner to loosen up from it, the grasp of what haunts an individual of why did that which isn't normal of the day approach. A form unseeing of a functional mindset to be engaging in one's present lifestyle.

"Vas, Aser, Vakero" Proclaimed the voice of a Power

Another blessing? entering. In Spanish, how potential yet unordinary. To such extent it was recognized, showing how good of an idea had it been for one to bestow on taming horses or knowing a trade. As how they operate and the potential to ride one is how he took it. What made this unorthodox was the direct fact that there was no history to the young man's life to have interests in riding nor taming a horse. Although there is high statements for knowledge on the skill to better the idol of oneself.

Without question, the young man followed to the gift and promise to go along with it. "A cowboy"? "What could the spoken verse of this blessing that came to be". Enthused, adjusting life in such direction.

Furthering the proper course to someone with such regards as to bless him with interests. It wasn't long in the week till an unexpected "Craigslist" notice was found on a regulated search page while looking for a gig. "Horse pen help" call was then traveled, hoping he reached the ad on time, picked up in cellphone. A door had opened.

A defining moment in recognition of matters so obtuse to aid a young man move forward. So the young man follows this triumph of voice and direction, ending up in an older women's horse farm.

She then a retired doctor, who decided to settle on her passion as an enthusiast and live on a large arced property out the country.

With a benefit of free housing in a small scale home near her larger sized house. All in favor as long as someone like the young man would help upkeep and look after the pen. Since her age made it more difficult to continue caring for her land and animals.

There was little explanation but there was also an option to live in another location itself. A house far off thee premises, It was a definite sketch.

A pond was in the back regardless with that was included behind the second house. The young man walked and realized how potentially wide view the power of who watched over him was taken notice of his progress. He didn't ace nor desire the horse pen job. Yet the options seemed open for him. With a accommodate and an acre at the age of that was revealed to be 25 years. A solid 25 years. A great age for one to leisure one would think, to grow and prosper with God Creator as his mentor.

Generously, it was in that mind set that there was more in store for him. House was adequate.

Arriving it was enough to be of sustainability. Then on to the back yard. Through a tall arrangement of trees, a steep traversal through them there was the pond like a sinister hidden oasis. It was both awing and something about it, definite in the direction of creepiness. Perfectly capable to plan a book to write or an interest in fishing. There had to be fish in there you could say. Although there was uncertainty to be the pool of amusement to last long. It was in place that the area as it was to be, A moment of reality was soon to take form. All was back at home as far as most furnishings. There in the main room, bed was set and Night was drawing near. No sound. Simply an anxieties peace of sorts. A time to breathe yet uneasy.

CHAPTER III
"SPERM EATERS"

LOCATION – Archdale, NC
11:00 PM Eastern Time.

Something wasn't right. To make matters worse everything about the place was both uncomfortable and eerie. Housing in the area was closer to hills and distant. There was nothing around really near the home in which the Lady had offered. Then there was the pond. It was way out back. Present also one strange street light simply lighting outside. One light pole that sat as the singular point around all acre.

The heat wasn't working, temperature in the room cold but not freezing. Yet something about the surroundings...was it the back of the yard or the peculiar pull of the large pond which sat past the woods. It was pulling and tugging as if it called out for one to come closer. Had the walls been supportive, alone asking was it a good idea to take this.

For the host to think it through so much. TV. Was left on, the house didn't creak but something outside DID! It was moving and it seemed as if it was creeping slowly. Substance was tapping the glass window. There was no dare to look. No one else inside the house but one person. It be damned if someone would try knocking at the door such late at night. No gun weapon ready but the boy would've been quick to draw a knife from the kitchen.

Ears ready to listen further for any sign of such intruder.

Persistent regardless without knocking a screw loose in the case his brain would seed a form of illness. A few minutes went by with televisions volume was set low. Nothing appeared further out the ordinary. A course of action was to rest and relax for a moment. Yet keep an eye open in the case of emergencies. Too much recently had spiraled out-of-control. It started with one eye then both soon closed swiftly. An aphrodisiac knocks him, A vision had occurred that instant.

The Dream.

An Arena of Rocks was present. Fighting between different adversary, one looked as if a stout version of "Marvel Comics Thanos". One other of the foes was a Genetic Muscular Orange humanoid with cunning appearance. One other was present but the facial features didn't seem into the picture to recall. It was outstanding any potentially glorifying of a show that could be felt. Cracks and energy surge, it came with sound! In an arena as if the start of an epic. All smiled and jerked at one another following a thunderous clash. Then in physical pain as if someone molested the anal cavity! sexually! while the dream still rolled and screeches followed! both disturbing and maniac. It was a form of rape. Another manner of embarrassment. Awoken the boy jets and startled! This was strange, disgusting and confusing most of all. After followed a man's voice in his head, staring around the dark room in the night.

"This is Gods wisdom" as if a level of sorts, right after disappearing. His lids yank open, After a drink of a bottled water it was even more difficult to sleep at night. Nothing was coming from outside either. No want in getting up and walk around the house, too confused and terror-stricken to even move an inch. "What the hell is going on and why did something tamper with me such late at night". It was difficult but the only thing he did was thump back to bed. With one eye open and a pinching nerve pain that something was still lurking outside with needs to invade the physical body in such was without a word terrifying as the experience. "Could there be something near the pond?" no understanding but damn well would not get up to find and check for oneself.

Again the night crept and outside became more of a standstill.

At last, an odd voice came along clamoring like an UN-welcomed guest at full moon. It was as real as the sweat of flesh came running with. A male voice called from inside the hosts head.

"This is Gods Wisdom" A fragment? Eyes pierced open creaking along the nowhere of estates. For only a single light was lit from outdoors. Only protection the boy had was his blanket and a lamp. ;If anything was intruding; in home it would be clubbed.

With little investigation. For even with confidence one would not go searching for things in the house that would further tamper the reality of what was it that popped in terrifyingly. Being damn too close. As if whatever spoke having been very near his ears enough to cause more than enough discomfort. If whatever were to show more aggression?! There was no more peace to fall back to the dark. Something was here and it bumped in the night.

With no sleep, Day opened and to realistic need it was best to leave. Not to mention money had mysteriously kept disappearing as if dementia of sorts took place. Or it had to have been something tampering with the persons coherence. Since it was day as off as the environment around him had been left. It was time to scout the area if anything had been misplaced or if any signs of evidence something was in the house. Checking the back yard, then past the back woods to the pond, scouting the area.

No recall if there was a pocket knife or any protection of sorts to walk along in the case of someone or something not meant to be here, prowling bold. After checking his vehicle, there didn't seem to be anything out of the usual nor any sign of the missing cash.

Regardless, it was best to walk beyond and double check the trees of the private forest, nothing. To the pond there seem to have been the exception of it still folded in facts that it was black, marsh like and very wide past its exceptional meticulousness.

Maybe there was in fact something hidden under its water. It was best to get out. Goose bumps rushed, the boy leaves and for some-time there was nothing of short of importance to acknowledge in fact this confirmed the worst was yet to come. Again, like a drifter moving out. Leaving the place behind forever.

That time would too seem peaceful and of focused ease. During that it went on that he relocated closer to friends and family. As a means to be centered and unprovoked to misdirection in the case of any oddity or unfortunate of events arise. People of faith ask why would God allow things like this to happen to them. Moving back.... it was told to him.

AS HE SLEPT A NIGHT IN HIS VEHICLE. THERE AGAIN VOICES APPROACHED.... NOW APPARENT IT HAD TO BE FROM OUTER SPACE BEINGS, AS REAL AS THEY ARE NOW.

Telling of what was here flying over his head, being simply, SLAVE-LABOR!, arriving to the destination like earth had beings eating out of their own piss and sperm with technological appendages connected in the brain to a computer interface.

Forced by another form of infection from world eaters of old. Being the rapid and updated variant of deep space exploration and stationary SUCKING of the cerebral cortex with as anyone's Grey and White matter. Scientist orchestrated from different regions of space, a master plan to document what was discovered! Gain control of other species and native people. Upgraded them as an ultimate gain of armies stretched by the eons of communication and elaborate diplomatic absorption of all intelligence.

To the farthest star the eyes could see. So many people being slaughtered, raped. Bloodlines removed from existence. How brainiacs got to a sophistication! Mayhem of murder was to no understanding the regret of the primordial biology that created this pattern of articulate details. Far from divine, it was indeed communications of signals and grand innovation that first sprouted from this movement.

"What or who else is out there". A familiar question as a foundation of elements to sees to it. Labor enhanced and control pushing the reach of normal physical, mental attributes barbarically. *Caligula*, gruesome, like symptoms of morons enticing the scripts of time itself. Life being betrayed of any Moral subject.

It took millennial's to where it is today. Just as cold yet controlled from vast amounts of old computers and new ones that resembled anything from basic root of understanding. Soon these technologies integrated onto their brains as a hope to see a door of an afterlife being a universal need. A need to exist Eternal!

World conquerors sought these things as an ultimate worships of One. Thriving endlessly to favor themselves and their drugged drunkenness would soon betray much of them. Tempered Scientist had taking revolts with leadership sabotaged from each root of the tree of this conquest and sophisticated network.

Assassinations, experimental bio weapons, weapon smiths all pushed forth agendas to DESTROY EVERYTHING that denied them a ground and a projected pace! Space armadas of tens of thousands of ships over the time accumulated millions more. Many inside these vessels died foolishly betrayed or hot headed to **see it**. Seeing, being the need of control for the eyes that motivated them. It was all turned into a sale and a line of who's next.

Judgment from brain absorption of new space and satellite authoritarianism being a ultimate manner in where one's life was tested and written. If not everyone's, like books of life and death.

Majority of Existence became encrypted onto mass amounts of servers. BIG NUCLEAR WEAPONS – explosions led as new golden calf. Bringing end of civilizations at a planetary scale. Star collapsing and gamma blasts that could be noticed from afar.

Leaving remnants of light and waves of energy dispersing. It taking the same powers that provoked such galactic pain, to form alliance and pledge oaths spanning Eons.

It was the peace that broke the mind. To manipulate the masses and distort beings, molested cybernetically. Sperm Eaters. Thriving in a black market of indulgence to extents of old men KNOWING, even the brain of an infant inside the womb of its mother was not safe. These things had been marketed. Now aging, with ethnics, memories and life becoming nothing.

CHAPTER IV
WHO IS THE EATER OF TIME AND MONEY?

Location – Greensboro, NC 05:00 PM Eastern Time.

It went on that after more research of the phenomenon, there we're very minimal like interactions. Lot of relocating, money spent for further personal peace. Nothing could be found, brought to retrace some steps. There was the occasional thought of tampering with the fact that someone was trying to further initiate conversations and give the host information. Forced. What seemed urgent, fruitful for need to act as if hasty.

""Donald J Trump is a DUMB ASS using satellites, a pact he made with occultist and necrophiliacs in The United States military as well as other (WHITE) extremists groups that wanted to seize control of the government using mass manipulation favored weaponized aero-space technology and media propaganda"""

- Voice

Shit..The boy would claim, "Why am I hearing this! How am I hearing this? Is this God with a connection to extraterrestrial?!" It seems very disturbing to be alarmed with such news of events. The Host being of Hispanic Migrant Mexican Background. It was at this point to be of the absurd and of a crack pot theorist. If didn't seem to be in the phase to be necessary to the interest to his personal life.

Although it was vital if it being true. "I need this to stop, I'm a busy guy". "This has to be extraterrestrial!, There's no way my mind is making this up" I shouldn't play around with this stuff".

As usual as the smart man being. Pulls out his cellphone, an idea struck to research in search of relatedness. Googled all if not most of it. Searches for use would be typed along words – UFO, TRUMP, SATELLITE, SPACE. Those we're only but a few to which seemed to aid his own personal study on the matters that were going along to which the public was too occupied to think of. At so it potentially opened the doors to the prospect that as selection goes. Random is the day although take root of it.

How could one balance such peculiarity. Some of the matters

pointed to high hopes and praise for such a random figure of things. Including to the eye of a 45th President of The United States to be of part of this jigsaw. "What are they doing to everybody, seeing how so hostile they've become in the open recently,". "Everyone has conversations on the table about these classes of subjects all the time". Paying rent and eating through money becoming a disposable lifestyle.

Kid Host became a valid Researcher and Foodie. Sleep hours were starting to be of a random schedule. All that mattered was that he stayed busy. Being comfortable to continue his personal life and other abilities to put these things together. Hostility of madness followed with voices coming back to tell him to stop researching and to not in irony as an idea to start writing in personal journals of any misshapen or of the unusual in his days.

A hammer of Voices disturbed him, filled with hate, discrimination, and of some means of like water boarding. "Don't open the book" ! They'd attack in a playful devious matter as well. By then, was of a formula now of different or multitudes of others convincing him in different times to be pressured into not placing such needs of "this" on context and written documentation. What ever this was, It did not want others to know of what information was being given to him.

Pointing different views to the notes that followed that are of valuable interest. Leading to what could potentially be for his safety and clairvoyance. "Man what did I do to deserve this?" Why does shit like this happen to me of all people.?' It wasn't a cry but a thought of a stone being tossed out its ground. Although as history teaches us.

When things get uncomfortable there's a manner to find the light in everything.

It is torture for a young man to be at such mania in his own home. "This is why I relocated in the first place!" Whoever you are leave me alone and get the hell away from me please". Carrying hope in words to shew away such pestilence, it would remain silent or roam in his day consistently. There we're times when the voices would to hold its place. Verbal attacks and insults, "Your going to Mexico". That rattled and hurt, For he was obviously more an American then that- which was accustomed to alienate another from their background and heritage. He needed to be left alone. He moved on to not taking it to personal.

There was guidance in his life, strength to never fall to such evils.

Abuse. A point was made and it didn't halt. It was eating his time and his income, Optimism a blessing, there's a way out of this stupendous riddle of things. He continued his personal interests and went out the house when he could to get air. Didn't use drugs or medication that would trigger side effects. A personal defense of his to the case it would be used against him. Becoming over protective.

Coming home from work a few weeks after the events. Laying in his couch. He stumbles into a deep sleep. It stuck like as if it could not have been resisted. It hit hard, it crept and repeated for a while. Hard working people tend to doze off like that, carrying two jobs at the time. With hopes to get eight hours of sleep. Part of a health routine.

Relocation to another area in Greensboro, North Carolina. As his schedule went, it didn't take long for a loss of comfort ability to be in par with his new mood that took stage from recent misshapes, to be at more peace over all. Living in the area was great opportunity to meditate and remain both vigilant, secured with the surroundings. Yet in this heavy rest a few days forward.

It again came into aggression to his daily life. A form of **Sleep Paralysis**. It knocked him while in his couch. If your familiar with this phenomenon, It has been researched to happen at random occasions to many people world wide. At this moment latching onto him startling. As the host dazed off, a language of something feminine followed, it spoke.

CHAPTER V
"I WANT A NEW BODY, CAN YOU HELP"?!

Location – Greensboro, NC 09:00 PM – Eastern Time.

"I want a new Body, Can you help"?
Host - Silent
"You see I want to continue and live like you as a human"
Host - I don't know how to help you..?!?

What follows in this sleep paralysis as "she" spoke ran in front of him a strange creature. It has two legs and two strange arms with no appendages added on, running straight at him! Revealing a more xenomorph body growing appendages. It shook so hard the host rapidly wakes from his deep doze. Nothing in the room laying on his couch. In that the way it interacted with his vulnerable state, was if it were far more real and disturbing.

The night was just as regular as the day.

Coming home from work exhausted from a schedule in the Summer Season. To be expected of such things was very rare for the mind to simply make all of this up. Maybe the crave for a women to be in his presence brought the devil to his home instead. He had a fling with a lady from the the same district educated from the University.

She would stop by every now and then to give him some company. What a distraction. She wasn't there long.

Carrying himself to bed immediately passing away again.

Realizing that it was the consequence of working two jobs at the time. The night being a perfect opportunity to lay back and play PLAYSTATION.

Schedule was to work early morning in his new found job as a Landscaping subcontractor. Puts a tole also with his second gig as a janitor in an office. Keeping himself occupied.

Following up the night another mirage wakens him. An Eye levitating like a mechanical orb!. Passing through his room like a ghost hovering showing off some detail. It floats in a size similar to that of a medicine ball. 2-3 feet in diameter. Color resembling silver and onyx or obsidian. It again awakens the young man. Terrified of this exposure.

Pops up! Slightly sweating in awe and dis balanced. Gets up and fetches a glass of water from the sink while checking his apartment for any signs of infiltration to his home. Doors Locked. Window Closed.

Bathroom Shut. Checks the time 01:00 AM. Nothing was shifted. It was just another night for him. Stranger things in life.

Waking up the same morning of the day that it all was followed.

His career was a mess, his sleep schedule and his luck seemed to be more against him. He constantly felt as if being watched and provoked. Things started to run their mouths at him, clamoring about how they opinionated of his persona. Now he, "Gods Son" as proclaimed.

Having felt examined all through his day and body. Never being able to catch a break and a breathe. It was the results of many things, stress, anxiety, hardships with these happenings.

None of it would make since. He worked payed the rent, sleep's and eats. Diet was lean and watched from his previous experiences of self imagery, modeling a few gigs along marijuana hobbies a couple years prier. Regardless he wasn't the type to entertain a crowd but was insightful in understanding to be bold in direction to his own goals.

Perhaps that direction in life was what caught. Interest from others including what was indeed in the outside. Remarkable thing of it all ;personal research and reason was an independent thought of what exactly was everyone else around him experiencing;? his neighbors as example, going through the area. They indeed too could be infiltrated by this silent invasion of personal space.

Entertained with the idea to ask questions only keeping them to himself, the host takes notes of any loose details from what the city being impacted of anything unusual. On his own, Strolling through the block in his car.

Aided by only a mirror.

- Are the clouds any different?
- Are there any markings in his body?
- Is he losing any hair?

No real shifts or changes although to simply put he seems normal to his physic as he is accustomed to. Changing of differences in that instance nothing through his glance being out of place from the usual. Yet as the days set orange and summer was ending a new season would follow. In hopes the day would be more tranquit, flowing like a cloud as much as what to expect.

Something of a horror arose, noises returned and it was of a cheerful attack of many sounds rising and moving as if coming from outside. There on the back patio of his home one night he walked out to again investigate. Smoking a cigarette. Carefully observant, absent of anything, but damn to the poor guy the noises were awful and obnoxious. A bolder voice followed as he looked around to see the deal while maintaining a focuses calm. Forced yet cool. HOST remained steady and ready in the case for a harsh jump. Something starts talking to his head, plays neutral feeling studied while being judged. Host follows and asks the heighten voice.

"Is this God? What's the deal? I thought you said I was to be expecting blessings! " Whats with all the noise and random appearances of monsters in my home!?"

At this point it is noticeable that there was a reminder of AN ENTITY, promising much to the young man. The boy reached the age of 26 that year. He waited patiently for the blessings of life to flourish while being bestowed by such character(s).

There was no answer from such abyssal lurker. Ever so absent, showing no image. That night haunted the hosts head. Piercing loud from screeches of variant noises coming from the invisible doom bringers seemed to have lingered dominating. No actual flesh nor proof of physical being. This young man would have acted so shockingly to such events. It was then out of exhaustion and annoyance the young man closes the door, walks back inside his room to rest and reassure himself that everything would be okay. It was looking far more bizarre, by the day there were new creatures in his life, popping in like a drug spot.

Feeling as if there was little to no privacy in his home. It didn't matter he had responsibilities to preform, the day after and all that followed was of his own doing. Wishful was it, slowly the young man came to a realization more interfering interactions coming that which shook, being God. It wasn't that this happened. Issue behind it is, that it acted maleficent and as if it lied. For something of unnatural decent come from out of nowhere to then mysteriously disappears over the year.

To only harass and act hostile while in his sleep with otherworldly followers is nothing short out of a nightmare and possibly he couldn't been lost In the senses. Thus his brain reacted as such to rejection and disbelief that any of this was real, that all of it was a freak accident. Something stalks in these shadows to only distort a man's thinking. To why the extent of how it seemed to manifest, in the way of of a horrible representation.

Obscured, the young man had a tie of different relationships in his past. There was someone in particular that would come over in visitations. She, too a now single adult, his last relationship with a young black women in school helped comfort and ease his outgoing American ritual of <u>work and pay</u> the bills. She didn't seem out the ordinary and when the young man needed answers.

There is the siren. Matron didn't know a thing about what was going on, it was a more self centered relation with her they kept things to themselves and they would move on. Young man already had eyes on his White buffalo. She was a beautiful women from Virginia, he adored her. So innocent of the pair, they got along just fine although they only communicated with text and phone calls.

She a very respected Lady among her spouses, strict in school and developing her interests in becoming a paralegal. Yet as the days went by she was stricken by his charm. A hardworking egotistic Hispanic male from North Carolina. His eyes aiming aiding immigration and labor ethnic as a means to support and be of a standing location in life. New, putting a step in the door for a comforting future. It was gonna take time and patients, they both had their sights on marriage matters.

It didn't take long for that to be in part of their dreams to follow up with. Like many other young men and women they developed a kind romance and as luck had it. It won them both. They romanced and grasped one another s time. Young man eventually wins her heart, "that women's crazy..", she dropped everything to be with him. She buys a car and moves to North Carolina they both envisioned a time together.

Falling in love, they begun a life a new and the days of peace

and joy was with in their time. She walked holding his hand and they moved together like one. He calmed his spirit and studied, yet the episodes on irrelevancy still followed his day, hostility was everywhere with this man. These problems of ancient evil still stalked the couple.

Deciding in these difficult endeavors going back to his roots in a career in culinary and the restaurant business seemed to be a better place for this circumstance of ever being watchful.

It carried a lot of mental stress along with, because of it, also now taking a toll on his relationship. It seemed clear that he was being sabotaged at this point. Left for dead by the things that summoned up in his room. No one called for this to happen but it was chasing and right on his tail everyday.

With this going on there was a decision for him to allow instead being forced to change direction of view and research topics on extraterrestrial origin and government military. Googling the hell out of everything the host now needed answers. Picking up more books at that point seemed small, having a hunch that he may be misled into further wishful information on these matters. Being doctrine details fresh and top researched.

Pieces had to be found and put together. Goal in mind now was "how the hell do I get out of this"?. Work was more difficult then it should've been. If not for the dimwit bold attitude and under-standing of how rare this punishment of inside conversations laying waste to him and so arise a deformed need to ask questions. Fathom-ing, learning to play chess with this devour-er. The Question of "Who are you?" always present. "Why are you here"?

CHAPTER VI
"WHAT IS YOUR NAME?"
WHAT HE SAW.

"FATA MORGANA" – A MIRAGE

Location – Greensboro, NC Time – 12:00 AM

"GOD?!".. There was no answer, not a damn thing could be cognizant to better approach this situation. As the host asked as to what now in turn?, Having confronted these specimens in discrete "mental projection". Repeatably questioning what the names of each of these entities are. They seemed to reject everything asked. Not taking him seriously of anything or what he stood for. These essence came in different varieties popping up in his head as if they mocking, studying, observing, spitting and cheering. It didn't take long to understand some of these beings carrying traits parasitic and foul of life, some coming threatening, distributing bizarre behavior. Others wanted to glorify the young person. As if it were forced into a blasphemous force of religious occult ceremony. "What the hell do they want from me?", opening doors have invited them for answering very little. "Just you wait" leaving nothing making sense of it.

Limited knowledge was given, as a means to keep the boy guessing. Chasing with delicate maneuverability being how rare this was. When that information was given, it seemed clear no one had the ability to tell the host a proper reply. As if they were both neglect and wanted to distort and taunt. Kind and well mannered the host would ask who they are and ask what the deal was for them to have caused such commotions. Proud and miserable at the circumstance there was little that could be done.

Understanding, leaving his love life out was the last thing he wanted to do but it had to be done as a means to keep his beloved romance with a sweet girl safe. When it came back to her she didn't approve, starting to reject and disable him, his goals. Losing interest at a perspective in both sides. It was very difficult to get her feelings heard, which is rule of thumb on keeping any relationship.

She hated him, feeling as if nothing was being heard. Loving but was so bamboozled by these things it was too intoxicating of an environment for the girl to even welcome this in her life. Naive, young and disruptive. He begged her to stay, would come back and she would go. He mesmerized as time went by trying his best to rationalize what was going on, Taking time and taking note of the happenings. Girlfriend didn't notice anything, There he collected in his home findings and resources to both write and draw what material, given up and what he could capture as days went on. Starting with what he saw.

There first was the conversations now echoing as if coming from his bathroom. It was preexisting at the time yet shouldn't be left undocumented."Strange talk" was being picked up as if it were all going inside his toilet. Three in total could be heard chatting it up as if they welcomed and knew one another well. Thee first of the three was a Lord,... a Rothschild, seemed he had ties with the figures who followed in topics of debate referencing to a new rise of players in the game of massacre in the Earthly world. A hot topic of them for what it seems. It was an expensive conversation of bickering fiends. Second of the group was a Donald J. Trump. They seemed to have some sort of connection with one another as to how the world was seen fit by a authority of "White Supremacy". Only mentions of agreement were said. Third and last of them was Vladimir Putin, of the time Russia's Prime Minister and image used for Public Service as Promised.

Main topics of ascensions and calling, as if accustomed in telepathic talks near each other, in an elaborate tune of spirits where were they. Privately in his room, random. Yet it was also noticed that they didn't trust one another and the host remaining quiet, only left his ears open to what they would say next. No seeming of alarms of the kids presence, strange and confusing. "What the hell was going on!?"...

Peculiar,

Of all things, Mercy shows itself openly, many would know not to remain noticed of such. These big players of a time, how could they have been in league of something else orchestrated. They didn't seem right, Something about them was stiff and different from what is accustomed to others views coming from the public. Yet what was the connection they had with one another and why was this conversation heard from within the mind all pointing to a WORLD ORDER. As it went, "The Gods have selected us" says the Rothschild. "It's this coming of age and conquest seems to have brought among their attention"?!. "hmm", says the conglomerate. Coming in, Bits of information gathered was of how thee Rothschild selling it hard. As if selecting his wording and autonomous in language.

Other two present, appeared silent and confused. Yet, they welcomed it and had no realization of the host's presence. Nor where they we're. What was said was faded in mystery to the most part.

Seems they accustomed again to converse with their minds or in some form technological. It took them minutes before they could disperse. Yet the young man took a while to get up from where he caught this blabber, being lying in bed late one night. Had it been from the toilet, a speaker box installed? Adjusts his lights and fixtures in the bathroom double checking, picking up as the way it did. In question, coming from somewhere explainable had there been a device hidden. Yet nothing was found.

Memory of such events was surely uneasy to recall, anyone would've gotten a dose of PTSD now expecting incoming conversations of mad man coming from a talking wall in a suburban neighborhood in the United States. What was the deal with that?

Notability having a strong mind regardless where ones perception is placed in dominate at all places. Showing no signs of losing himself he still continued forward into finding it beneficial of perhaps rewarding. For the forces that held him back seen viciously ahead.

Foreshadowing of what was to come was drawing near and it was as followed. Thus the man's story of disgrace, displacement, fight, heartache, torture. Madness and piety. A Christian made Atheist made Agnostic biological makeshift of an image.. What is it?

After sometime he started getting into looking at the sky more. It wasn't in hopes to summon something but more of signs and indications of life elsewhere non human of origin. At least not of this planet.. So much wonder looking towards the heavens. There were always stories of extraterrestrial presence reaching all over media.

From different drones and craft, to the most noticeable highlighted found globally. It would reach news outlets, giving much excitement for some people. Our own approach from those in our powers to actually inform better, wouldn't release a damn thing about them. Forcing everyone not to pay attention or as a means to leave the topic alone all together. Urban lore, Young man saw his share of things and stories went truthfully as far as the ends of the world.

Double checking everything, selective of bestowed knowledge simplified as it could represent, Showing itself. Some day's things were there, other times nothing seemed present or out the ordinary, as usual. When these presences placed themselves in his life he had his phone and attention ready to capture as much detail as needed.

After all, there were just to many things associated that you'd be a fool not to pick it up and adjust the view for others to see. Up night after night...

Morning came, getting the idea to go outside and redeem his health since being accustomed to being in bed and waking up later due to his concerns with vigilance. Up late grasping thoughts emerged, eyes open if case of anything. Grabbing a bottle of water rushing out the door. Leaving with need to still look up. Then there it was, like a shining orb with a tail. It was a ship of some sort peeking and sliding forward at mornings rise, right in front of his path. It swings to the back and disappears. In a time frame of five seconds. Its all that was present but only a few clouds.

He in shock, Yet continued to finish his routine to run out in neighborhood. As the day went on insisting to describe and note the story to his loved one. Then Girlfriend and best friend. She didn't look encouraged or pleased. Yet supportive for him to continue being present with his goals. Regardless of how much he had to adjust it on his life and career. There were things still pushing him to follow up on this dilemma. Thee dilemma being that where ever he went they would follow and push him. Like bullies, "No life's" he recognized them. Yet there were a hand full of intelligence to aid with his focus. It wasn't the best situation for the young man knowing he had that toxicity behind shadowing. Motivated, his books and charm, gaze on what was necessary for development. Writing notes and saving tasks the man worked hard to research. With possible efforts to fulfill whatwas necessary for others to take notice and even correct him. It was all in his head and it was assured that he wasn't a schizophrenic.

If checked in this modern age, most would say he was crazy. Too needed of a doctor and treatment. He was balanced, meditated and went searching for God again. In Prayer and in faith, he felt the presence of his savior would heal him and answer as to what was wrong having been the centered interests. Called and called and called, days went on and nothing changed. If anything the voices would come back and laugh at him. "Leave"! I'm in prayer. Feeling rejected, claiming now the God that answered him was a pest. That it was disgusting. "Leave!!" they'd return. It didn't. He worked hard to connect properly without any disturbance. They forced themselves in his life.

Wanted to be comfortable and without being pulled towards this now toxic crowd of mutants. Then something of a alter interest steps in. "Don't worry little person".. says a third signal of thought. It wasn't god but it sounded like he wanted to take use of these events and take hold of these situation. It was near miracle to be able to pick up a comforting force, scaring off the demons. He couldn't fathom what it was, yet acted as if a shield, moving off. Uneasy, this could've been a whole another monster of its class. 'What are you?" The boy asks.

There was no reply yet the giant of a character smirked and went on to stomp forward in its cause. Behemoth in a man's head, tutored to extent to preserve one way or another there was too many things interfering alone at home. A "Fata-Morgana" of peace present. It was then spoken that the formidable figure being aliased "The Giant Robot", <u>pacts made with white supremacists in the military. Only acting in truth a Trojan Horse.</u>

It was clear it had to be brain projected to see things. For if one studied the cause of characters it had to be from a technological advantage of distant power. Nothing else placed effort to show itself, Although the "G.R" had power to illusion further. Placing strategy. An example displaying its presence like the statue of its own in a room full of other illusive projected critters. They took turns both initiating charm, laughter, sensuality even homosexuality towards the young man. In the mix there was an agreement to use him and take turns. In a communications web of complex roots. Further interaction without sounding any alarms of what laws placed this endeavor of oddity routine and illegal, domestically. Harmful. Like a hologram show of random animals did the stampede of things vanish. Potentially other aliens even Artificial Intelligence designed characters to pressure the kid to flee hysterically.

So it went on, now the truth in fact the host being caught in between a disaster of aliens. With everything coming in from some original designer or another. Mutating and interfering with the public very openly. Had the kid been a tool for a secret dark occult of monsters. Every voice and figure now insisting he listen and witness to everyone's tales and needs. "I promise you'll get something out of this". Was a consistent answer. Abusers, At that instant picking up notebooks and a pen scribbling down was a good action making obvious sense to do so in the case this interaction would go far from neutral. These characters got too comfortable with agonizing the kid, hyperbole of episode's always all different from one another.

"Having no time for new friends, new adventures." "How the Fuck do I get out of this".

Laughable.

KITO's LAW

"Search for self mortality"

To live immortal, you must feel pain as mortal, Flesh"!

KITO

Do not stray in robotic's as a form of longativity, Biological exsistence is the only life to live"

Do not manipulate your people but instead, offer solutions of open talks & allow ideas"

Ape kills Machine"

Machine should never kill Man, nor harm"

Never test a Star, never play with its elements!, this is beyond possession"

Never harm a beautiful person," Never"

When in doubt, test a prostitute"

As a wise prophet said,"Blood of my Blood Flesh of my Flesh"!

CHAPTER VII
"RULES OF THUMB"

1. If it is intelligent, then it must have strategy.
2. If it there is life, then there must be muscle.
3. If It has strength, then it must have history.
4. If it has written then it thinks.
5. If it is mammal, then it must have a thumb, for creation.
6. If it has a hand, then it must have built.
7. If it built, then it must have structures.
8. If there are architectures, then it must have had battle to erode them.
9. If it had war, then it is aggressive so on the defense.
10. Aggressiveness has flaws and downfall.
11. Perfections are limited, time betrays it, thus aging and weakening.
12. Does it Thrive on another existence.
13. What Does It Eat?
14. How Does It Eat?
15. If It isn't human, It must Die

Mana

"I thought it was seaweed
too, but it's actually".

"Composite" (waste)

"Giant Robot Cockblocks information
fostering rapid colony"

– In 1963, Roswell had become
a "state-of-the-art" Contamination
center for found extraterrestrial
craft, including "some given".
Had it been for a small
team of military police saying
no to trusting them. They'd all
be dead & vanished. Some said
yes to everything. Including kissing
their feet "when they get here".
Manipulated.

CHAPTER VIII
"WHAT DOES IT EAT"

RULE 15 – "IF IT ISN'T HUMAN, IT MUST DIE"
~ THUMB RULES OF KITO

Aged rocks and abundant sources of helium, hydrogen with older elements. Formations of DNA, Atomic particles fusing and manifesting as one. Hard and soft, magma flamed and rose. Fauna sprouts, encouraging life to develop. Fundamental Microbiology and bacteria clustering together to grow, evolving. It spread, Grew mouth following with taste' So on. In theory, there is just cause to suggest that when one is hungry then the eyes developed to "look". Eating has always been the primary just cause as to why we exist. To Hunt. What we hunted with our eyes gazing upon, is a true element of feasts. Our interests became business and pleasure to rise above the scavenger. Feeding on anything with discipline much more, grace.

"Don't put that in your mouth'. Its why we don't eat what isn't clean nor flavorful. Being raised modestly we are taught certain things as a basic foundation for the clever and rational thinking as all traverse the ever reality of living it further. What kills the human body is bacteria in the stomach. It contributes to many of life effects that further multiply and ruin ones physical health. Isn't yet scientifically spoken open about, although evidence and research show wise that these facts remain true. Clever science has shown dependent on what we consume. When forth, that the way the body manages itself to cleanse naturally flushing whats buried inside. Drinking lots of fluids manages waste and carries out whats collected in our bowls, even recycled saliva. In fact its what they ate found of oddity, those dwellers beyond the stars.

Meat blocks. Made from days in a lab, What these eaters ate was sperm. Some of these foods included insects blocks and vegetation blocks. It was science and survival. A means to fast pace laborers on new worlds then send their built ships to orbit. Also, unfortunately for some now absent of proper food supply, having to live underground escaping a collapsing environment. This is research given to man. Countless episodes of information passed from one being to another like "students" as they called others like the boy. Yet no teachers but the A.I Operators behind them.

These entities were extraterrestrial who mastered, labored, pushed an agenda to envelope with distant star engagements. They, monumental as it being having to devise means to hibernate and eat as they slept while on deep dark voyage. They had pumps on their genitalia when they arrived on Earth and found by man of military and science. After careful study it was shown they were supplementing off of filtered urine and sperm as protein. No sign of a blend for taste or powered ingredients to at least make it any better. Its what they had and survived off. It has been the only means to go on a one way trip to one planet or the other even with limited supplies on different lands harsh terrain.

After and autopsy of found entities, having God made differently. Cyborg, unnatural, Stomach bloated as if filled to hold its only burden. Theorized as a means to carry its otherwise secreted element for years long travel, regurgitated. Intestines small and straight only stretched out to 4 feet or so. Compared to human at 15 feet or so. structure in height was at 3 feet 5 inches. Fingers long and narrow.

Eyes black with lens, Technology as imitation to frighten was primordial reason. Also as a protection from sun emitting differences. Limiting damage to the pupils. To watch things in the dark. A world of VIRTUAL REALITY. Their bodies laid stiff. Nervous system left inactive. By the time they arrived to the scene others cautioned for disease and radiation hazards that for real reasons wouldn't be for the better interests of ones safety to approach.

Precautions had to be made. They would lift their arms and hands towards their mouths and ask for something.. yet it wasn't understood till a baby boomer military police proclaimed that one of thee first entities needed water. Far voyage from its origin along with instruments found to be attached to "its" entire body had clear indication that **IT** was parched and of need of liquid. Thirsty.

Where was their origin was a question of everyday presence. It was also clear that a consistent stray of proper documentation of these entities was not well established. Committing that others in American Ranks in the Department even made communion and contact. A dead body was present but so was a live one and it spoke a mouth full. To how these conversations went along and if they even got far was more closed doors and left to the ears of a few selected. What ever the case was it was clear the guys who came malnourished to be excused were not of this planet named Earth's origin.

When the world shook of how God created many things. It was a question of which God was it? These entities were noted to convince of "Creator" that it was also disgusting and inside everyone. Yet like many foreign talks. Miscommunication or errors in dialects would have misguided the formula in what these principles of religious views meant.

As far as the gaze of stars, Thee night sky is fearsome. How acute is the task to move the people of a land. How major it must be to move the rhythms of a living entities heart beat. Which heart beat? There's always a grasp for things and a need to control is both barbaric and foolish. Physiologically the expanse to want to know, is how to get to it and how to keep it thriving alive or killing it.

SOME ATE STARS. It was a space conquers prize to engulf portions of dark matter found to be an isotope of sorts. Artificially even from a world non other than construct of computers. Beings that approached first were a sight, what controlled them in their own sense of chemistry was a clear understanding that they too had Narcissism. Business to them was formulated out of abuse and sabotage. Clear indications they too were accustomed to drug use and some other unknown elixir, maybe. To keep themselves wasted and

captivated by the small talks of what was in the mists on colonization even hostile takeover. They, a flurry of information present of
studies showed adjustments. Different characters, others in the
chambers of shadows, its need of fruits and drink with eyes closed
lost in fantasy.

There are the "Birds". Chanting, ancient ever so full of song and
rhythm. Beautifully elegant. Yet in outer space the birds were both
respected, feared, admirable. Pale skin and found dressed with exotic
fowl feathers. Disrespectful in extent, given knowledge of how fond-
ness of another, kept the boy captive in an aviary. They too used
computers to monitor the captive host. In his home like a cell. All
knowing, historic in recognition, some claim it was a testament of
space and its tactics in selling ascension or afterlife. Many who
approached the young student scaring the shit out of him for laughs
and giggles. Very comedic noticeably organized.

Possible information given to him by some other beings in the room.
Spliced Homunculus, Non other then crafted life created in a lab.
Some were men of different places, promised new bodies as a retire-
ment fund of sorts. They were mostly picked out of those that lived
fast and rebellious, having culture of their own. Some birds were
made the skin of white or blue. Both hues respectfully representing
of Honor, Masculinity, Respect, Loyalty to their Creator and Leader,
moral driven. Young men selected since birth. When many saw how
twisted they've become of themselves a name tarnished like samurai
made "ronin".

Remnants of what was left behind there too being Mafia style leader-
ships and communism, a base of what societies had the authority to
speak with the young host. Outskirts of their reign collecting and
absorbing brains data, used as espionage, population control and
farming. Manipulated entertainment satellite/ship arsenals preexisting into the future, kid being in the middle. It was all around us.

Thus what you probably saw growing up watching television.

Things in the sky? Did God send them. No there was clear indication of things other. Other being them, or so it seemed. Birds coming in we classified as Grey. Recognized to us as Blue too. This had to be necessary for others to know who was in some of those Unidentified Flying Objects everyone talked about. Slaves? Yet who would care?

Having to cater to a life he had would anchor the obvious he had to do both. By force. So there was no other way around it but to work and listen while telling as many people as he could right before making sure to double or triple check some of those details. It was a labor of Hercules to handle the pressure of it all.

This was given to the host over the course of time as he witnessed these objects for weeks turned months that went by. Silver metallic small circles, tic-tac objects. Hard to drink this sort of thing, being eaten alive. There was a market in the sky and it was us as livestock and play things. The military wanted this kept secret and quiet, a private uncontrollable party in a Mexican migrants home. It being entertained that because of that status, a young man without laws that governed his rights and protection in this country. American Military and espionage departments happened to have been parked at his home. Selling and buying into it, regardless an inhabitant.

Intertwined in the subject of the happenings here. Using remote access satellites fusing his life and body to a computer his relation-ship had little notice of it. Now kid on a sale. It was Ishtar given weight.

Things steaming up between Ukraine and Russia at the time gave notice to persistent anxiety in all fronts. Not to mention American Military wanted first dibs on this. This meant fame, fortune and the power of the all divine.

Eyes that could see. Ears that listened way to hard. They went mad. Colonels turned mad men chasing everyone who'd catch a glimpse of their tooth fairy. Their little gate keepers in the night. They protected their privacy no matter the cost. So as long as they had a taste. This the boy found in Prayer, it stalked him for who knows how long before a start into this circumstance of things. Thus the savages came.

"GOD, WHERE ARE YOU? IVE HEARD THE VOICES AGAIN FATHER. I DID MY BEST TO CONTACT YOU, I HOPE EVERYTHING IS ALRIGHT. IS THIS THE PAIN OF KNOWLEDGE BESTOWED? IS THIS NOT ABUSE"

"Sir, (laughing and chuckling continued).

"I'm sorry to tell you but as much as you want.. you are a special American".

Some one popped..., the boy thought.

"You were being used for experimentation to be fed to extraterrestrials to see what's inside them, what's connected to them"..

"Their vessels anyway"

"We've asked them to leave you alone but their not moving" Boy crawling back to bed asks,

"Who are you?"

"This is the United States, this has been very useful to us." "You were used as a program, we believe it being God"

Boy knew it was a sale. It crushed him but it did not matter. So as long as he wasn't pushing it, he wanted out. It was too distracting and hurtful as a young adult growing with this burden as it felt. Attempts to communicate with anyone else felt consequential of practice.

Then a third appearance of a voice proclaiming to them shouted in interruption.

"They put the voice of creator in a box"!

"You know where they got that information from?!" "Absorbing your people"!

"With our technology"!

What ever was going on, It wasn't in a situation to feel at fear. It however would ripple the effects of what would also follow.

Obvious enough, noticeably. There was the hint of caution and anxiety. A third interrupting party, clearly again wasn't of Earth.

Someone made the formula of how the young man became a host in the first place. Forced to witness and be taught secrets relatable to our surrounding habitat. Playing a character such as God. A reason that these gentlemen here became so close as to speak with the young man in the first place. Intelligent to know of the American speaker(s) tone to show they did not want to be noticed. Yet never knocked on the door to ask questions.

"We've asked you to leave, HE IS NOT FOR SALE!"

Says one military personal, the third entity without a reply. Nor seemed to care to what statements had been enacted. Regardless

indeed there was a trade that was explained and caught by the boy. American men who seemed paired and uncomfortable urged them to let him be. Wasn't properly taken accountable as to how he would be left alone knowing where he lived, what he knew was important. He would not be exiting.

It was urged for host to see, and listen. Some time went by and it was placed for the boy to find himself. Aliens would not listen to the American man's advice. So forth was communication telepathic, which in regards was an attachment to his brain, from either technologies.

His mind could not put together the happenings. Which part became heavy and a chore of a hell to solve. It was tuned as part of their alien economy of human existence.

HAVING BEEN DECLARED A STUDENT, for being open to the conversations, drips of secrets as a reward for finding a wise mans treasure. His prayer hitting the spot of something, someone, a group of beings maybe. Yet there was acknowledgment that he was meant to grasp as much information of what was given if not all. To write it down. If not by force. To take it as a promise, some otherworldly perspective, a poisoned drink that had you suffer differently as a means to open a seventieth and eighth sense. A flow of autistic intelligence. God awful twisted benevolence.

He was TOLD TO LEARN. TOLD TO KNOW WHAT WAS WRONG WITH HIS HOME. HOW MEN OF MILITARY WERE LIVING INSIDE EVERYONE WITH A WIDE RANGE OF SATELLITES ALL INTER-LINKED. ALL EATING OUT THE ASS OF ANOTHER. A human centipede. That was a military secret of what was happening a reason these guys were never shut down totally and never opened to the public until further investigations had to be made. Actions in bases and command centers. Hidden deep.

Being nervous at such haste declared weakness, Absent of fear, so what was the boy nervous about? Kid had to remain strong. These technologies on Earth devoted into brain alterations showed the instruments as he was taught had to have beaten out of portions of his brain. Fearing of dementia or other side effects. From such religiously invested space instruments penetrating the skull. "Speaking of that, was it ever studied...as far as the side effects?'. "There's nothing to worry about!" "Although I will admit that those men in military are disgusting. You know they were going around eating all your people in a gulp!?"

'A gulp?'

"Yes, that's who was here by the way. American military, the Army!" Disgusting! "Que asco"! Stating it brief and laughably like an impish creature lost in misogamy. "Some of them would show themselves pissing over a city or pretending to finish masturbating over it. They didn't care"; "To us it was horrible and were very sorry for what happened. Also some of them from our networks hate you because they don't like humans and hate that you know too much now about "New Bodies as they call them". "We're all accustomed to eating out of your heads for some time now son ".

A message given was obvious to show forth. Events, they weren't naive. They knew it would mean war. Not to mention the timing.

Humanity being in the verge to announce their presence and credit the achievement was entwined to devilment believing that if other life exists. It is advanced, for the most part -nice happy people- ! We envisioned to think so. Such silliness, to believe advance life as "just add water, innocent sea monkeys ".

Singing songs of praise with the United States Military. In the mix of the days many of these people surrounding him now noticeably coming from a Cold war extremist agenda. Executive powers and legislative knew very much of the boys circumstances. Stories beginning to flout around the senate of THE EASTS COAST infestation. Laughable and thought provoking in both angles. It would be rude to pervert another nation knowing how they've gotten along for so long without a poisonous thrive for absorption.

Space force had begun overseeing our population, them having a rough start with uprising details that the new structured branch had already been infiltrated. By the roots, foreign and domestic fiends in the shadows. Potentially making a toxic mess of things. Being responsible for satellites, this strategy of ultimate surveillance would soon doom everyone. America now honey combed by a tactical

"Nationwide network" with secret brainwashing capabilities sold into.

As history repeats itself, *a wiser army knows higher ground,* some of these entities displayed formidable movements and unique designed ships in Eastern Airspace. News soon sprouted of "metallic orbs and objects" in other nations.. For one instance there is fear and speculation as to what they do. Lurking in the dark. When in the day the movements displayed as rare and always drifted or left as a cover up.

Some masses have even welcomed it, in Christian tradition, as if to integrate the mindset that they are here as <u>Gods Angels</u> to man kind. Many ethical issues are present. They've developed means of superior space and exploration technologies doesn't mean they know any better. If any it shows that they are more prone to invade and expand. Need had to be present for these instruments they've been researched to have traveled with to be formulated. Need is a standard in the drive to aggressively push boundaries and wants of things. It's real and could be classified as theory. Yet when there are claims and spoken details of a black market having information of human trafficking as an otherworldly result, passed around the room. Problems rise from these traits and behaviors.

These things are real. They've been found along with the military and god knows who else thriving out of lives, programming our heads was just an addition to it all. Further details explain that's what their doing here. Expanding a dangerous and evil market. Other civilizations being failed of a case. Placing ours in the mix of it.

Seeing us as another Jewel of a planet and its people a delicacy of artificial experience. They had their wealthy class, or elite engaging its people with these technologies as they nested on a city or area near scripted.

Integrated radio frequencies from the ground up to bounce and link to one's nervous system and brain to see, taste, feel as we do.

Cellphones increasing that gimmick to a 90%!, that's a 90 percent of what the brain is capable of producing. We had been in their clutches for some time now, these details being directly given to the young man taken under the very wing. Very unethical and consequence high in motive of it.

As continued, connected, they had themselves embark and sleep in a cryonics of sorts while venturing space. Jumping from life to life, feeling and tasting. It was the height of a fucked up excellence to needy and ugly as they soak up space radiation in a luxury planet hopping experience. It was damn remarkable these guys felt like pimps because of it. Controlling and manipulating the lives of hundreds of thousands of men, women everyday some of them almost an entire lifespan.

Brains in a box. Feelings stored in a server since child birth, memories of virginity's sold in a cybersex network. Bodies molested. It being a disgraceful presence as to why many other now nations motivated themselves in a space agenda. As well did some of the needy on Earth rising human treason to the highest degree. God knows other planets started embracing it.

Many private trade partnerships with NATO being introduced.

Human-alien-sex slaves and children offered, being a prime rib for the guests. Everyone was doing everything to give them what they wanted as it was programmed. As it was meant, in hopes to be gifted intelligence and blueprints.

Unwise, we as civilians being out in the open being fed "them". Privately as **forced sacrifice.** Banks we're called out of comfort as a prime example of who knew about it. How the world labored in human existence when old, as a secret means to get closer to the young and beautiful.

Humans wanted in and it broke his heart to know the fiends have surrounded personal space. Everyone on this wanted to get a grasp of documents supporting these details and grab as much of all the money circulated. Had been for the use of needy personal interests.

Promises of more advanced medical, weapons, ships, radar, thievery introduced.

Hostile take over as if invasion would be healthy. Then the ever hungry satellites and space arsenals that absorbed us. Now afloat and being shared with brain suckers. Cloud storing capabilities had been hacked by all. Soon to be a demise, WANTING TO SEE IT.

"Well it was wrong,
but to us these
moments we're everything.

"(Frog)"

- In reference to being
inside someone elses
body cybernitically

- Big guy in the Universe
(wealthy)

Gift

CHAPTER IX
"THE RICH AND NEEDY"

Making matters worse, hostilities were everywhere and our military prostrate to accept them in secret, their behavior. Embrace it and indulge with them. Already connected to their cerebral cortex, everyone's eyes had experienced BLUR. Lying every step of the way as to what they were doing or why they were doing in the dark "means for better good". Promise of bedding beautiful women hypnotized to sleep with them. As long as these entities got a taste, suckers for pussy. When no one else took notice or saw anything for such long periods of time left as an excuse.

Truth to thought it was clear indications they wanted control of our steps in investigation and how to promote themselves as Mortals, Gods, progression of religious identity left perverted. Boss man made owners of flesh and child. Some of these entities falsely claiming the work of another theirs, as a totality when only small steps were included in any strategy or plot. Occult's would then be seeded and enhanced out of sacred practice and praise.

Groups of wealthy elite from around the world needed more. "IS IT SAFE", now a key word to promote if a presence on another is welcomed and no one is watching to masturbate inside us. Like rape in the middle of the streets. It's how everyone of these cowards was now comfortable enough to promote themselves.

Members doing so being in league with organizations as the fabled <u>Illuminati</u>, Flocking with mobs everyone got a boost of techno power from these ships, up kept like pocket gods.

Enriching tacky, these enhancements to the understanding, being more overlooked and closed mouthed in conversation.

Punitive problems becoming angles of thorns placed to prick anyone wanting to get closer to cracking the mystery. Putting criminals down for Justice was more rare with the illusion of entitled Gods. As they looked at one another together, Siamese twins of human traitor and alien leeched brains, bodies and living.

Family branches and bloodlines of the most modern money men. Bank influenced, oil tycoons, steel and automotive. A combination led them to increase the strive for notice and acceptance in communities. Taunted, chased like our host. As if the kid had answers to what they needed. Tools like the military played them out. Keen examples of money laundering strategy were eroded, it was typical. An example being present was an abuse of power from Men of high ranks.

There was no image to upkeep if its influence representing a farce, leading with misleading. Especially with that yearly budget congress offered. Once it hit and was split, that money was left with stains and samples of residue. There was only a fraction of time that it would take to disperse once the military got a finger on it. Portions being directed to the Russians as a gift and an I owe you present, in reality even with so many Tariffs and Sanctions.

Scamming the people of any real examples of economic translations giving way too of false media.

A ride of exceptions to trade were going up as going down in Wall street just for looks. A market value never changed as in the cost of expenses was indifferent. They didn't even have to touch a reserve they'd have held up. Saudis got a taste simply as a bribe to get them satisfied with taking cover as a relevancy. "As long as they were there'. Being ones bitch you could say, while ever confused fuck killing off whatever was in the east. It was said right, yet the return from it showed error of flaw for puny motives that would only last a decade at its best, as a red eye of embarrassments.

British being present ever so anxious of collapse. Yearned and grunted for being mishandled in the ways of respect. It's Intelligence being paid off like a land lord. American patriots would've been in tears. Pushing all strings and being a primary source of influence. It was placed upon them to help "kill everyone"every moral or dialect that was misspoken to thee ears of a night fiend. placing themselves all over as long as they could target what pleased the force of distasteful pleasures. We being surrounded, not at one point did this enter their mind of thought as to what we were enclosed with.

It was obvious, there being a bubble in Modern society. A creeping and a crawling was a working class coming. If Information had legs, it run from what was behind it. There being a layer of interests was of societies in need. Elderly seeking Gods wisdom in its betrayal of eternity in Darkness. Regardless there was money pouring into whatever class of notes to riddles there was in search maximum level restricted so called information. Whatever heighten it anyways. Middle Class in America had been disrupted and forced into a poverty level. Not one mouth dared to speak of it.

King of the crop was those who knew everything.

The host collected this information as it was pushed on him. Day in and Day out is what was placed upon his journals. Much of it being more of a custom made complex copy and paste. Knowing many in the world would've wanted in on this. Spanish Gold, how could've he gotten paid from this at such a mesmerizing of defected ways. There were ideas given to him that seemed to be of highest expense. As in simplicity where many would indulge.

Had it reviewed in truth, the satellites and space technologies over our heads programming everyone and everything under.

Controlled and monitored by traitors and aliens.

Yet where this being pocketed was difficult to enact to such open radiance of what now all over the boy. An audience full of simple and wrinkle. There was comedy in it. From a third perspective of things you could imagine such frustrations as to how attractive that made one so pushed with ideas and knowledge to be absorbed by what's around him. Utilizing every tool in inventory to take and claim for oneself. There was gold abundant in the lands. Kid was marked a golden calf, Very much defamed.

When the Spanish sailed to the new land. They carried with them all kinds of precious metals and cloths with details only origin of ages from master craftsmen would know of where to add. It's the high class of things. To which one thing is placed or evoked in touch and embarked. It takes bloodlines or wit of rule breaking to formulate results, there was arrogance of a sailor during high storms being told not to sail out. In this life you have to be bold. "There is to be gold in the sea near the coasts to which one would've considered closing to port in times that long ago". Those ships as example, some not making it, left and lost abundance during horrid episodes while out in voyage.

Offered the where about of Spanish coin and other locations of such prosperous interests of treasure. All while reminded of what else had been present around him. What a toxic scenario of conversations being told in a room full of disgusting old figures, murderous mad men made pawns in the first place. It was told they used their own special equipment purchased from military in the United States and others to contact and listen to how they moved in the first placed. Linked to the boys brain had escalated to a mass of computers and other top secret gadgets other wise putting him in danger. Cybernetic hacking into the skull using technology had been a science fiction for so long.

I inform it to be real and more aggressively implemented publicly in shadows. Being the boy in the middle of such events being rare. Made the obvious of need to study him forced nature. Involving him in a honey pit to attract and eat out of. No matter

the military making its way to pinpoint as needs to take detail and throw the kid under the bus. What information was it he was acquiring? There was no phone call made to figure out what was going on to him directly. Yet some of these fruits of information being exquisite in taste and allure. Secret organizations and aliens had poured answers.

"Thee pyramids were only truthfully a thousand or so years old." Referring to what was in Egypt. It wasn't built by slaves but by workers and a payment in bread and beer. They even had carts with sails familiar to boats, flowing and moving in sand dunes like ocean wave surfers. Drifting and running though it was a means of fun". "Atlantis was more of a heighten sandbar that was stretched far off into the the apparent Atlantic Ocean".

It was popular then, that they established a market in those sands, placing them far from where it was predetermined. Some time later it collapsed due to weight in which the sand bar itself, could not hold long after the mass of people vending moved in and out of them. With that there being market stalks, all those antiquities sank and washed away some sinking, some deeply hidden from age old movements of the seaside. Lost as tales, these age old questions being answered showed high value profiled information for many. Being indeed what was important for human footprint. That is our ancestors, our history.

There being answers to these things, of what was left for us. Placed on the notebook papers to finish later. As impressive as it was, indeed that finishing touch of things to execute excellence onto his work. Some fun facts, it was rooted to implement later as a dire understanding to public of what angles these illustration might aid in the coming future. As complex as it is, visions and animations of oddity hitting many corners of interests, pored like a fragmented pieces of surrealism.

Narrative was then placed from the host as he continued writing and narrowing answers of what these beings passed onto him. With the United States military of hands enriched with whatever was possessing them. It was subject as if an importance of sorts. Without denial it was clear they wanted all of it. Smiling inside his head watching a screen manically. Enveloping the man just like the E. Ts with space technologies to hack and look into ones perception.

Executive order, misdirection and hate, subject set to enclose and control of the young man life and decision making. Leaving the host young man fighting it off and focusing on his own agendas.

Hes loved ones kept at bay and of need to understand what the circumstance was. What was attacking him? Crying, confused trying to comprehend what was wrong. No one understood how he was being afflicted and provoked. Signs of suffering from a sort of mental illness. "Get some help'! Is what was said to the young man.

It caused anger and frustration. He was in heart with a head on right telling like it is to others. Hoping more would bringing about the proper steps to handle these situations better. The truth being that Aliens were talking to him directly with some means and he was being chased by the United States and some programs to follow up with it. Encouraged to absorb, isolate and take recognition of whatever notes and work he was inscribing. It was without a doubt a part of human idea to move forward, Needing help. Asking for aid from these abusers was rational start of interests, problem had been how to interact with the public without panic.

Rejection from natural will, of things from such amateur character was obvious. These happenings of normal accustomed ways were of course to root around him as a means to take hold. Everyone was being mind controlled. It feels like your being pulled by strings yourself, no one could escape it. Hearing details and scribe them of how a young man being taken out of his comfort zone. listening to the feelings of a monster in the attic wanting to "show him stuff" and encourage a form of teaching but in these manners there's also the obvious, scribe while in flames.

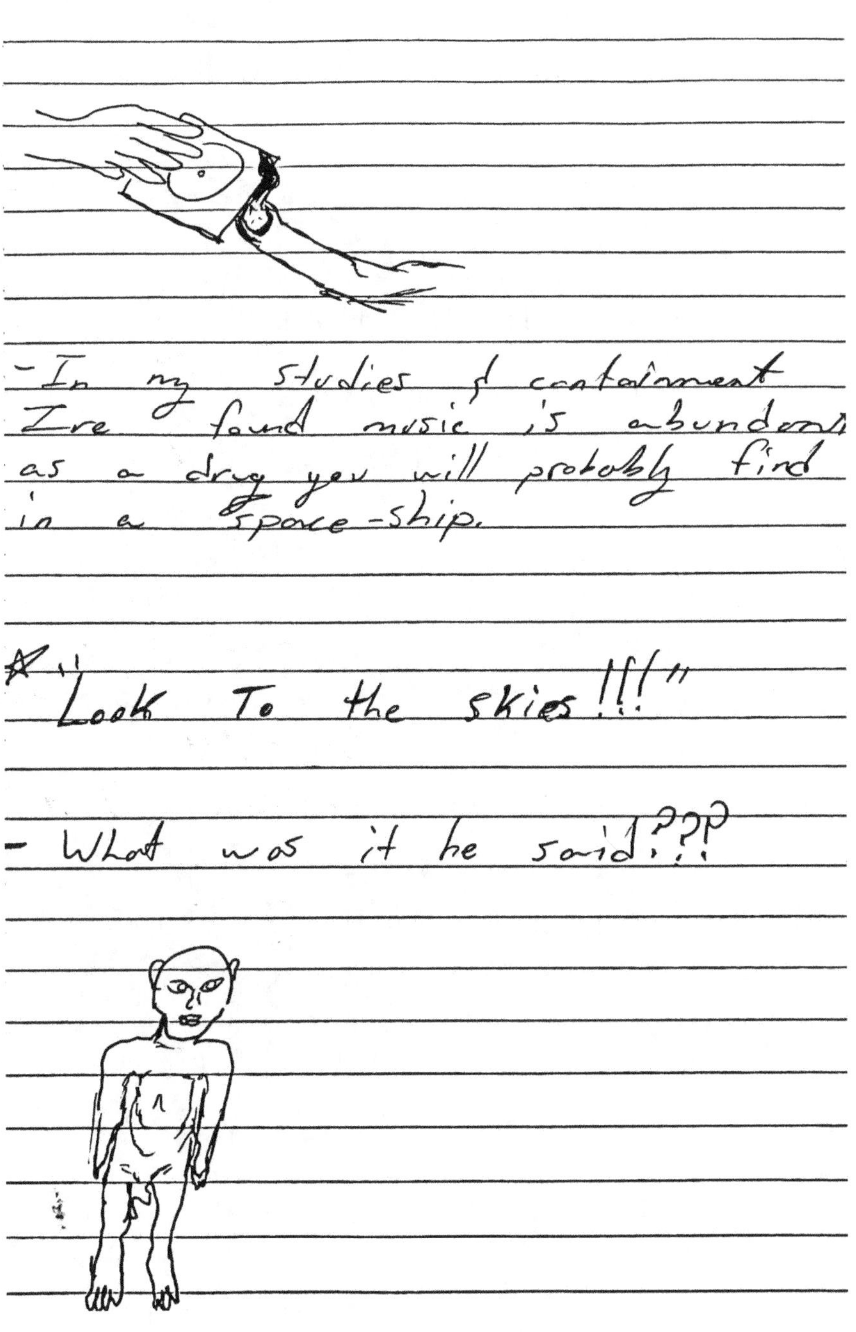

- In my studies of containment
I've found music is abundant
as a drug you will probably find
in a space-ship.

* "Look To the skies!!!"

- What was it he said???

CHAPTER X
"LISTEN TO ME, WITH ALL DUE RESPECT!"

There it is!

"The root of all evil!, It was them." How quickly fingers being pointed was as subject to the tone of aggression from things always in the offensive. Children being born with altered birth defects, identity to modern day from the cause and effect of genetic miss-code at the core in the womb artificially mishandled by foreign intruders". Homosexuality being a mental illness distributed by space hypnosis. Cause of, *experimental weaponry enacting brainwash*. Male aggregators from *a far* attaching to children and younger life. Human sex trafficking cases being rooted, United States Army along with private companies using resources to enrich a now cannibalistic secret program. Endorsing at a nation wide level feeding someone else in the dark its <u>wants</u> and <u>personal needs</u>.

It was there. Project blue beam was exactly as Canadian journalist "Serge Monast" claimed. Real testimonies of a scandalous mystery program where science was used by the military in respect, to procreate as well multiply alien clones (*biological findings from wreckage located*). THUS THE FALSE INVASION of human society in a near future. Human Ovaries breached by Introduced sperm of foreign life and vice versa.

Clones underground being breed then injected in their own ships as labor. At least that was the plot for control of Earths future.

All costly to the funds both delivered and stolen by officials claiming Uncle Sam's image. Being found to be flawed of real interests, everyone that knew anything outside a circle of members had been hunted by everything. It had been those in Arms that wanted this exchange. "Manipulated", simply wanting to see something. A sense of Misogamy, Only punishing themselves.

Having been the wreckage itself been a trap to further applied labor and purposed re-engineering by the intruders themselves.

So comfortable of a more leisured life, many of these established members of society -funded- aided in eroding labs and facilities to progress this endeavor in the Antarctic, even Alaskan territories *multi use camps*. A "sort of lazy behavior" demonstrated tampered infantry from *something* while in test facilities.

Had further discovery noticed an entire program maneuvered as an actual alien invasion set to control these entities flown on our orbit, launched by our own trusted best. Given ships, technologies surgically added being brain implants. Basically antennas.

American Military had a hard time getting back what they set free all over the place.

Brain implants. It was that then aliens would control them with their own hidden computer systems and overlapping units radar and hacking signals outside of Earths atmosphere. Many of these satellite clusters and systems had new laser fire weaponry meant to defend the planet. Having it all be a failure in all fonts. Aliens controlled the signals and the secret codes capable of using them. Laying waste to whoever they'd desire and enforce their will on our planet. Controlling everything with an antenna even the conscious thinking of the human race being part of the formula of bug invasion. These beings had studied everything from the start.

Problem was some foresaw this, thus was the actions of sabotage and ploys encouraging us as community to fight back at all costs. Being watched, out of control. Mass surveillance on everyone having computers and screens, it had not just been the National Security Agency or CIA piercing through our homes.

E. Ts had manipulated the cause to the extent of phones communications use and camera monitoring. They all we're watching us, even if you had been engaging in pornography with your cellphone, this pests, hot and red looking back grotesque at everyone with a face time camera installed even the back one..

Everyone who questioned or wanted out was targeted including same men, who as order enacting in military authority. Already battling broken ties and relations because of implemented cerebral manipulation from other space entities. Creating a **Domino effect** of struggles to everyone else in front lines fighting. Infantry near the areas of secret locations. Guarded and lured to leave as twisted people if that. It took decades to produce things, creatures even, you think filters could stop it from the mind progressing evils and yet it got worse. It didn't just cost money, it laid the life of worthy great men whose lives died in vain.

Putting a foot down and pushing reason. Such then Serge Monast who gave his life for us as a means to inform public interests, echoing ours to prompt more detailed investigations on military deception. Dying of psychotronic weapons. He really died from UFOS and government satellites targeting his life and body similar was as the protagonist. He pushed it as best as he could. How dare they attack someone with such disrespect, to degrade him for speaking up carrying his values and beliefs. These things were obvious space parasites. Scavengers even, it was regrettable to inform how deceptive these predators took control of everything and everyone.

Satellites had back fired, used throughout the cold war to linger onto the human population pushed from extremist who had been adjusted in power. Humiliating themselves and human brethren onto masturbation orgies the extraterrestrial threats pissed for. Physiologically breaking the darker man onto a musician or athlete as examples of a computer interface advance manipulated script. CIA had already run manic dropping drugs in the "hoods". Forcing kids to sag their jeans for humiliation, mass maneuvered onto society becoming popular instead. Damage had been done and no one had been arrested, investigations had to be necessary.

It had been the pinnacle of *Classified Government high life.*

Knowing all secrets and control of experimental satellite technologies. Seeing how simplified it was to trick human conscious to portray oneself by the fever of another. Men in Camouflage and other attire started caring less about what they wore. It was more of a push of the envelope and fast money and power by destruction of peace and prosperity in American Cultured Community. Like Amateurs they had targeted women with an erection needy of pleasing, lusting and mad. Slobbering while their brains had become burnt and shrieked to a glee state of pain by their Alien Masters. Had they, their stomach been growling all their lives to be so hungry.

They were eating out of us. How dare time and space of things allow growth of such hostilities to maintain disasters towards people in general. We were losing ground on this and oath keepers of these post laws, were In the way of growth of men and women to be enlisted effectively. Taking off the damage of these chaotic misogamists. They pleasured off of murder and rape at the most horrific from age old need to "see things". Formed human occult's to upkeep the desires of their masters.

With the military as an expendable to pay for anything and everything they wanted. Including wealth of these occult's and special interests groups. Thus was the 'Illuminati issue". Being told they all knowing of the secrets of eternal life and youth if following commands being pushed to control and harvest for years that would follow.

Thus was their betrayal as men of honor. As long as their bodies were striving another day they were more than happy to oblige. With most of it a makeshift and a fail of things. Much of the information in place from these so called foundations was including blueprints of weapons. *Psychotronic-Psychotropic,* expandable to disrupt even further.

With that started the market of human information harvesting. We weren't alone on this. Yet it being undeniable people being hurt plenty. You could notice small changes in human innovation and popularity. Selection of Artists and Media had been orchestrated to control the population. They wanted the kids. They needed the children's attention to be focused on the "good and neat stuff".

There has been young teenagers and children led onto accidents.

To be of discovery that older monstrous and perverted men for the most part had been inside a young person's body discretely swallowing feelings and emotions added some control of independent lives and thoughts as a taste of youth. Giving no care of whatever side effects could these technologies produce on a nation wide scale. Dementia and tinnitus being examples that something was taking a hold of your ears and connecting to the brain. Things had groomed young girls to be whores later as a use.

There was so much pain, in the place. Including NATO, other alliances as well as spy agencies, causing disasters and wars all over the world by manipulated aggression. Experimental brain altering Weaponry being culprit. Given and traded they used it, a hyperbole of powers to traitors running it. With that you realize and question "Where do all these terrorist and militia get their weapons from? Guns and ammo, missiles, aircraft.

It was a deal breaker for white extremists with hoarded money sitting and chatting of who's turn it was to send the Saudis problems to kill more native Sunni's. Those arsenals being found by a "clean up crew". Boy scouts being hand selected, a clever tool enlisted from the ground up. A couple years in service to the country or even guys and girls in the law enforcement. Those being rookie expendables. Sent to reclaim it without full brief or what it was they we're doing in the other side of the world.

Mysteriously vanishing, being set up by none other than the same Country's departments who sent them. Reason for that?, They started knowing "Too much information" as they put it.

Information that would lead to the top of the pyramid scheme monitored by idiots and space aliens. Back to the arms they found?, It was a matter of who gave it to them rather then why do they murder with those tools. Population Control was as it is a disaster.

These extremist from western powers and other private affiliations thought it would be a neat idea to sell it to them, common arsenals of all kinds. In real hopes they'd kill every ethnic group living in eastern areas of the World. Extermination of anything considered *non-white* or near its interests. LIES PRODUCED. Tempt even the devil himself being programmed in world assemblies with something unknowingly hovering everyone's back. "We we're hijacked"! Was a main excuse. Goal was simple It wasn't clearly "stolen" it was implanted!, This they spoke.

With cycles of similar patterns found in different territories. Everywhere, with some pacts moving these weapons simply to impoverished or disordered human life they already left behind. AFRICA for instance, simply to kill them off by the means of themselves being weaponized and the mind being irreversibly disrupted. Simply to have blacks killing blacks. While the State Department and other branches together with favored goons watching everyone from inside their heads and satellites connecting brains to screens with teams controlling the suffering, "Kid, What is this."

Secret Oath keepers, keepers of secrets. It was a mirror of the same. There being countless recognized phenomenon the world just didn't get. It was bound in a rhythm of rinse and repeat. As these occult's and book tellers aged. So did a corrupt science of anxiety bestowed onto the day they could walk. As far as who was able to afford these information's anyway. To hoard and be the only to know of such details was a war itself. Monsters with suits and daddy's money tycoons. Space entities controlled both the Government and the Rich. Promising Eternal Life and Luxury.

Monopolizing it even. Advice was a given yet it was never the correct formula. "Don't listen to them", "Take a plane and run away!".

As followed madness took hold of the same talks and extravagant voices stalking them. It invited a dilemma like no other in the mid and late 19 hundreds. End of the second World War followed with the space race. Russians aimed to please.

Americans we're lagging behind. Yet it was enough to notice it as motivation to build a ladder and match it. When strategy came to play during the Cold War eras. It was told, cause of it was fear of mind altering telekinetic powers, research and decades of friendly fire with UN-conventional war mongering in the world.

A secret battle of space threats led to much discovery.

Offensive Tactics had been left punitive and not in our favor.

Finding the cause of such damage harming a commanding officers life Ironic. To take a breathe being a blessing itself this was a civilians unique luck.

Space threats are who pulled the strings in everyone's heads. Only answer was to "Nuke the sky". Being the logical answer to stopping alien monsters. A plan devised by the so called Elite and mysterious powers. Either efforts seemed futile or it just never happened. Whatever epic, they allowed for them to prosper. Surrounded by weapons we had already given, Earth Honey Combed by intruders and space technologies.

ICBM weaponry proved minimal, a rapid exercise of what little they could do. Surrendering to that extent was an only plausible outcome. "Why didn't they use more man power or tell the world?!" The young host would call back to these entities. "promised power and women".."That's all they wanted".."knowledge of anything was kept behind closed doors, every excuse used." No other way to see it, - Human Traitors and Men of Dishonor-, being obvious formatted puppets consumed of fear kept it to themselves.

Other nations around the world, along parties enforcing next level steps and procedures. Around the clock. Pamphlets, being a subject as a hand out. Those handpicked individuals, in new created pacts and circles predestine To 'know it all' was how they would put it. Would continue producing the new days movements on a saga. Doctrine, followed by hidden details that were passed in rapid shuffle of hands. As well as orders on how those involved see to controlling the world.

Little knowing how small it was to catch up to advance methods of espionage these entities used. Even these plans being laid out, along much high security they included. Structured to a percentage of the form as a whole. A script of sorts from the start. It was branded onto military and others minds to catapult these details like they did from a get go. Scrimmage had been the effect yet never played properly to confuse the enemy.

Like it went, it was strategy being conducted, mentioned about and carefully examined before execution. Aliens watched it all from the eyes of those few who knew the entire thing had "something connected to them" the entire time. Like a second head on the shoulder. With minimal indication of other presence in the room. Traffic over years of secrecy was monitored and picked up with ships inter- faces. Kerosene in a Rocket just would've been scarce in extreme efforts of space retaliations.

You could only imagine the face those men now colonels probably made realizing how much they had already surrendered to those cybernetic creatures. Wishful Friendlies, taunting everyone with comedy. If only they weren't parasitic. Meanwhile, The boy kept writing these details as best he could. It didn't matter how sloppy the information was adjusted down, it was more a matter of actually doing it. Gazing at the stories at parts in real time.

"LO ESO PAPA"!!

Encouraging the promise of progression, it is futile to escape the inevitable.

"Vietnam, what happened there was the USSR Soviets and a prompt alliance of the nations were fighting secret battles. They figured they'd pick up secrets of God". "Russians retaliated with impalement to craft, from decades past'. As it's understood, there were locations all over the world these entities would go hide and lurk. It was defi- nitely Boogeymen".

"Russians showed evidence that some of the locals were seeing things, including going missing." Villagers were spooked speaking of monsters there. Wasn't any better massacre was brewing with a new found hysteria of communism. Ask, Why did we really go to Vietnam in the first place? Says one of the voices from the ship? "No kidding whys that? What was it" says the young man. Entity dry of an answer.

"American Military took its own case at it"! 'Started sending teams to investigate first followed after the Russians'. "Men were lost and didn't recover from physiological and nerve damage'. "Ask how did near over one million United States trained men end up dead with many others wounded?!" Did you know we manipulated the women to murder and men rape". "Even the pot holes and tactics were proven useful". Coming to the brain like a reflex. As if already built in as extinction of surprise attacks. The militia was taught cybernetically.

Campaigning on Vietnamese Soil was a mistake, costing a record of over half a million soldiers lives not to mentioning casualties. Without disregarding civilians, others who still needed accountability. Simple records of that even showed great failure from the western country. That was Vietnam alone. It left an insanity plague post war. Had it all been registered injury and left people coming back home with something still holding onto them. It had been the brain altering ships and satellites meant to destroy good solders and veterans further.

It was information only the rich and expansive knew.

Expansive as a thoughts focus to absorb all of the land they sought to integrate plots and solutions. Books, Notes found in historic landmarks, Details of stories picked up from the mindless tricks of oddities. It was that which then gave them need and gluttony to eat as these entities did.

To find truth and power. How deceived lives were placed at things claiming to have answers. It was that where realization how far and low they all went to acquire tastes of knowledge. To know things.

Investments were found to have pushed global affairs to aid and contribute in their fountain. Story has it, many elitists ran to this "signals in their head". Alarm ranging to meet and greet, killing for it. Fucking for it. It didn't matter. With enough wealth from European and American Banking systems to finance world crime and reduction of how these pursuits gathered both allies and enemies in that circle. American Army was hot for these things.

Thus an established pact of white tortures who were amassed to amuse and entertain. Entertaining that which spoke to the host.

Horror of *Cthulhu, Mythical space God of Madness* that would bring answers to a Christian. A reason why the Pentagon In Maryland with architecture to stand as it is built. As was told, "To ward off The all knowing need and eye of Jesus Christ, Father". It was a fluster of information. The etcetera that went on for years as little details emerged to a random selected figure in these toxic fortunes of old chase. There wasn't a clear answer as to why choose a young man in North Carolina as an apprentice. Yet it was dire to understand the fabric of realty on a person, but what seemed as a limitless amount of important characters here on Earth.

Wasn't just a Grey Who'd pop in. Regardless the communication being rare and formulated in pursuit to have hidden history doctrine. It didn't bother him as much until an always so bastardy thing sets in and disobeys, Moral ground. To leave people alone. It just wasn't there for these pests and people to leave humility react at a maturity to call. What would've saved time for these influences if they've remembered to use a cell phone.

There! another artifact is there captain!..

Reaction of action was needed. Flight or fight? With whatever resources the young man had it was to flourish in basic writing in pen and paper to document these events as nourishment. Analysis of those notes was important and it was there you could find some use of it. These things were dying of thirst to eat of whatever was given and redeem it as their own and witness in a small room. With the army as a disposal to these elite it was clear they all had the same agendas in mind and it was clear, these methods of doing, being a standard like committing thievery of a private matter.

Without a doubt they were using satellites and other instruments to do so. Mind reading of a sense to an extent where there was little air and feet to stretch oneself. Manipulation as a whole. So best course of action.

!TELL EVERYONE!

It wasn't difficult for someone to get their heads in a twist of things. There are serious number of filters the brain has to go through in which the switch of the mind comes in play. For groups of people to surround someone with space technologies and just stare and swallow all day and night.

Being accurate of things as far as how share of intelligence is both passed and given. There was numerous reasons to believe much of our in charge of Defense and government, noticed these foes in the mind studying them. What makes people tick. It was again Cold War programs that prolonged for several decades.

Possibly forced driven. To think the Military was making deals with these shadows as offerings.

When the young man was given "too much information'.

There was a command spoken aloud to these extraterrestrials that he was "not for sale'. Making it sound as if they were accustomed to this sort of behavior. Offering or convincing entities with so much to say in the form of fact to give human rag dolls. To squeeze or at times play. Like they got off of it. So confusing and shameful. So confusing...

"Babe! Get up!"

His girlfriend would convince him to get up at noon. Working in the restaurant industry kept him afloat while being bothered by Military, State Department and other agencies whom made deals to study together and take advantage of the young man and his life while isolated.

"Give me 5 minutes I promise I'll get up"!

"Hurry up because I'm trying to take advantage as much as I can of today before the day's over.'

"I have to go back home Thursday morning"!

"So Get Up"!!

His girlfriend would visit him with her living out of state. She'd drive just to get closer to him. She was in her early 20s getting ready to aid the public one day as a servant and law abiding citizen. Online School studying her roles as a future paralegal.

He'd speak about everything to her and although uncomfortable she still loved him. Having a spunky attitude and character while holding him close for comfort and company. Yet with the government on his back betraying his safety. As well as hers.

It was complicated for anyone to understand especially her, this information he'd share with whom he trusted the best. She hated it. It ate up whatever time could've been for the two of them and devoured much of whatever time together they had. She a Christian girl from Harrisonburg, Virginia. Gorgeous and independent. Darker skin complexion with her Great grandparents coming from American Prehistory slave traits. Stern on biblical belief, having a wonderful personality as well as a heart.

"SO COULD YOU PUT SOMETHING ELSE ON!"

She says to him one morning a week she visited. "What's wrong with my outfit?"

"If you're gonna go dressed like that then there's no way I'm stepping out with you"! 'No disrespect babe but I want you to at least try."

Giving him a familiar look of anxiety, gift of love and peace for the young man.

With both chuckling...

She understood her loving man was suffering while walking in life together. They two committed. Worked on cutting the pressures of knowing so much and burdened by reality of something or someone always stalking and shadowing. Always silent when she was around. These entities were predator and waited for opportunity to absorb whatever they could out of the time the two being close to one another, unwelcoming powers of computers, saving data of their time.

Extremists goons commit into intoxicating their day without burst of random anger and acts of depression, a mind hacking attack. They betrayed them, When being closer and harmony holding each other..By others, there were the groups of military who worked in secret with organizations and occult's. Always a feeling that they sucked him like a straw. Knowing how to utilize these Alien technologies to live in our bodies. Like unison.

Attached to people like parasites and night predators. At times controlling the lives of whole families. Secreting them of their own time, money by superstitious beliefs. Using Religion, Moral and karma as a choose of integrated assault and plot to pull on an innocents life. Different families had too been targeted, from decade long history the list went on. Being foul played by these Space Entities and Department Branches. As to the most part, like the young man with his Christian Beliefs. Had it been the challenge he was promised so long ago now in prayer.

These pests were into this sort of sexual nurture to chase civilians. Not to mentioned some paid top dollar to hitch a ride on another person's life on force. At least while no one would notice these groups of ugly. That no one would know how they all were indulged, eaten alive and harnessed, utilizing space satellites and hidden technologies targeting everyone. To attach to a person with a cellphone in their pocket independently.

Followed by absorbing brain activity with massive computers and space antenna. There was deep and private information stored and shared, some of these computers weren't on this planet for the most part. Whatever we have here being punitive in comparison to the "other" alien mega scrapers these entitles eroded. In truth it was all hostile. Now perplexed in clouded focus, It was an unusual form of unity in the couple with marriage in mind.

Surrounded by machines and monsters who sleep inside their bodies. Natural emotion was starting to lack. She simply could not fathom the turmoil he was undergoing and her being vulnerably more emotional than him being a man and her being a women. It was without a doubt a dangerous situation for the two. The pair had been both a host to a traumatic space and military threat.

Aliens and **Military**, inside bodies masturbating and mating as one. Inside everyone as part of a secret deal from the pentagon and other branches who've embraced the activity.

She couldn't notice anything, It not only took a toll on their life. These fears and conversations he'd share with her. It was toxic for the poor girl who was innocent from this. Having nothing to do with it in the first place. She only wanted a stable life with him.

Damaging love. His eyes closed. Realizing how disrupted and destroyed a life with her now had been reduced. 'Leave us alone'!! multiple times the young host called out. When it came to having sex they both appealed to one another. Both carrying years of history still pleasured each other's emotional and physical needs.

He would disturbingly close his mind during bedroom time with her. She would undress herself and displayed a body for him. Black young Lady from Virginia. Long legged, beautiful face and smile. When he held her close to his torso, she would look back or open her eyes to find his not being able to stare directly at her.

Doing yet his duties to her as a man. It damaged her still. Not being able to interact as a loving couple. Being in knowing the two were being disrupted by sex deprived maniacs. "It's gonna be okay", her answer.

After a week was over shed pack her bags, wake in the morning they'd both touch lips. Gripping her thighs. It was difficult to relieve her of time away. Have her things ready and drive all the way back home taking near four hours at times. She did it for him. He loved her for it. They both working together to spend more time with one another in more fruitful days that blessed by their creator she'd join him in a long life as one.

Playing music of all interests to captivate and aid his natural escape from it. His waterfall of reality and monsters who seemed to have defiled his heaven. Walking as if they crept in illusive tactics. It was tactical, a different path from what he was promised now months ago by a voice in his mind who spoke as if God.

There was also strategy. A simple liking of music in his phone is what kept him alive along with his loved ones.

Music there had kept him captivated with the sounds of independent artist. They seemed to all be calm from that, monsters in the attic. As if all these entities wanted, was his time. Share of music, control of his love life the need to see what happens next.

Now that those notes stacked themselves as books. Very limited time being present with ever growing anxiety from that which prowled in mind. Lost voices, formed forced bound with what now felt like conjoined twins sharing his body. They wanted him censored and controlled.

Taking a more comforting career choice. Eased up more opportunities for him to find some peace out of what now was a dire problem to his life. Being able now to survive off of an environment along with the check, food being bountiful. It saved money at a cost of his looks. Growing fat. Only one judging for his more lack of appearance from what being accustomed being confidence never broken. Challenges that paved no road to his success yet an all seeing eye being present maintained both order and chaos. It is someone's lust. Lust to see men suffer.

There was no way, when these things happen. With forced to being taken advantage. Not a chance for that to win his day.

Looking back at his women. With a consistent thought he kept to himself...

"I can't let this happen to other people"!!

"There's just no way I am letting this things control my life and peace.!"

"What can I do next to alert others of how much of these things live inside our heads with space technologies!"

How bad deals in the military with aliens left human hostages by force for long periods of time. Thus was the Story of Kid, a true pioneer in the ventures to the unknown. Facing the odds of everything around him, including the ancestors that betrayed us, here and from out there. Eons of drunkenness with computers have made cybersex parasites. It took the rational thinking of many to find the means of keeping the world safe from hostilities. As well the acceptance of information from the stars and the heavens.

Finding the reasons for the riddles in the first place. It is, oh so undoubtedly malicious.

CHAPTER XI
DANGER MONEY

His girlfriend left him. She went back to her mother's even
after begging to stay...

Racing through a grocery store, With his first book of notes in hand. Walking in such a pace to not seem out of place. There was dread. His ass was in trouble. His wit was out of place. So where was his God? He ran all over the place pretending to stay calm yet dazed and confused.

"Dammit"!!!

It seemed hysterical with such impression. Running to an older women, in hopes she could hear his cry!

"*Hey mam!*, I believe my life in danger and need someone to continue with this book of information I have..."

Like the saying goes cat got his tongue.

Stops his tone, she looks at him bewildered. What the problem here is was the fact he in better interests is better off handling his book of information to a more stronger figured person rather than a helpless old lady. Tossing over instead, next he accumulates his focus and pushes to hand it to a larger guy in the store. Stood at least an inch taller than him. Host being at 5'11 or so. Initiating a better make of talks and convince the man to listen.

"*Hey Sir!*, I have a quick question to ask.!", I have this book of research and need to give it to better hands in the case something happens to me". I'm being chased around by government personal and aliens I think wanting my information."

Man looks at him at awe and asks. "Are you sure..?"

Regardless he shakes his head and agrees.

To some relief, He hands it quick to him and bursts out the doors. Walking Faster then when he was inside the local store. Hurries to the front of his car door. A 1995 BMW 328i convertible. Jumps right in and moves out the parking lot onto another location he felt would be better for him to gather himself up. Moving from one parking lot to the other. These things that spoke to him now more aggressive and out of place. With sounds and tones that made no sense of anything. He was being tortured, forced into punishment and water boarded.

YEAR - 2016

LOCATION - Havana, Cuba United States Embassy.

A String of attacks is alerted. Relations escalate between Chinese, American and Russian Foreign policies as well as fellow nations in a circle of espionage. Over three dozen accidents reported cases of diplomats and others are attacked from public records of what seems to be a microwave attack. A phenomenon known as the <u>FREY effect</u>. Presence of loud noises, ringing, buzzing and grinding. Some stealth attack of sonic weapons.

Seeming to be present also. Professionals point to the possibilities including and not limited to direct attacks coming from satellite beams. No one knowing who did it.

;Frey; itself being a Neuroscience expert who first studied the symptoms himself. Displayed that these afflictions are the cause of sonic attacks relatable in tests, to have left those victims in Havana with *brain injury* and *damage to their ear canals.*

"You know too much!"

The entities screech back within his head.

"We don't want the children to know what we're doing here!". "It would ruin everything"!

"What would your Christian fellows think of our actions"!

"Get out!", the young man cries while pushing the gas on that BMW!

"This is bad, I hope my notes don't go down the waste man." "How the hell does this happen to me, of all the damn luck" "To think I thought it was God…"**"Fuck it!"**

Coming to a gas station only a couple miles away.

Further action to call his family and friends for the first time. That he indeed was in trouble and to alert them in the case something does happen in a way now endangering his life.

"Tantas estrellas para andar conestas estupidesses."

As he stares onto the sky in broad daylight outside the vehicle. Looking back at a narrow glance he puts his phone down after communicating with everyone in his circle. Decides on the hit or miss on calling an ambulance. There just wasn't anyway he could reach a hospital to check himself while in his traumatic conditions. Taking one big breathe moving to initiate it.

In fictional stories and other lore passed on. There is always a Protagonists. Some along more like anti-heroes where they aren't much of saving lives or others but more a personal story of themselves. In a combination of unity in those structures of a person, It's a strength that includes survival of means of Mental, Spiritual and even Physical tests. Where in a time of place they do become needed. How much of a task of endurance pushes against one and elements to ascend from a problem. Strength to beat the odds and master it. A mastiff of a challenge where yet it's been tamed.

"Hello, yes I called about wanting to make a report"! "Can you tell me what the problem is?"

"I am speaking to you as honest and truthfully as I can be.."

"There are *UFOs* and other *military affiliates* stalking me with satellites and I think drones communicating directly to me right now." I don't use drugs and I don't drink alcohol *much*". I'd like to make a report about this."

It took an immense amount of strength for a young man to open up about this more publicly. In this age certain conversations about these things ;a theory behind hearing noises from the back of conscious; made you a suspect to a mentally ill state-of-being and certainly unfit for society. Risking it all it was time he *grew the pair he was given* and do every approach alerting others in the case maybe this was the start of an attack or alien invasion.

If the lady on the phone huffed and puffed, it was regardless now, spoken and spread to others to know more. They needed to know.. that important. In his mind people needed to prepare themselves. It fell on him with so much pressure to continue.

"Please tell me exactly how you're hearing this and I'll send an officer to speak with you"

'I believe their using satellites!"

"I understand what your telling me", "but I need you to remember to remain calm, and the officer is on his way being there shortly"

"Last thing, I'd like for an ambulance to arrive at my location"

After a brief message of information was given to the 911 operator. It was only a matter of time for the officer to appear at the scene. Making sure he didn't seem out of tone. He reminded to check himself, Hands weren't shaking. His voice was confident as he reminded his tone used during that phone call. Prepared and engaging enough for whatever aid, in hopes would appear on time.

Police arrive shortly after,.

It was already late night and there being one officer on the property gave a lot of relief and brought comfort. Officer steps out the vehicle. In all the gear the boys in blue arrived with. A darker skin toned man approaches in front of the young host. There being need to tell him everything. It was in the back of his mind. To tell him everything!!...

"Hey glad to see you here!, says the boy.

"Everything OK?"," We were told that you are having issues with things talking to you in your head and that you feel your life is being threatened after. Without too much time to continue the conversation more patrols and an Emergency ambulance finally arrive. Rejoiced, He rejects all questions further to the official kindly and joins the other crew who jump out the larger box truck vehicle. Checking...

Moving ahead, he's in what is believed to be his death bed. The ambulance takes him straight to a mental hospital. His book flat front on his lap. A man had approached the emergency respondents and handed it back for the reason it was returned. Like a curse it didn't leave his hands. It came right back. A solid drop of his heart to see the closed strapped leather journal the writing was embedded in.

Not realizing at first where he was, there was only pain pushing from the top of his head. He sat on a chair and communicated verbally of the accident, to those who appeared in front of him being three or so workers from different positions in the building. It was then after a blood work transfusion, that the

nurse and staff left. He started closing his eyes tired and drained. A show was about to commence.

"What am I going to tell her, I hope she's okay"

"This isn't what I had planned out for us. I WORKED SO HARD. Making sure we'd be safe and happy"

"Not to mention she risked it all to be with me, I love her so much"..

"Even though she went back to her mom she still calls me." "I wonder if there's anyway she knows I'm here."

As the young man tries to wonder with his eyes closed shut, A pain unnatural to his migraine of sorts develops. Like a laser attack from different angles, a nano-millimeter sized laser moving inside of his brain straight down from the middle. More or so his eyes shut, with so much panic induced in him. There was little energy left from running. *Please leave..* I need you things to leave me alone and get out of here !". He was under a strange mutilation remaining silent.

Yelling from atop his head yet remaining silent from factors that would otherwise alarm others in the building to rush in. Could potentially for instance sedate or even strap his body in a chair.

Exhausted, pain still from within his cerebral. If it wasn't any worse there was also the noise of entities at the misery of it. As if they we're drooling in laughter and fetish.

"I want his body!".

Commands from some leader of these parasites insisted to malformed his conscious as if to infiltrate his body. Through whatever means in a haste. Needy.

Paying no mind to the boy, telling them to remove themselves away and halt whatever action they pushed onto the brain he carried. Only Agony could be the word from the core of what was happening to the young man.

"I can't leave her, I'm so sorry!". "I can't fail my baby"

It's never shameful for a man to cry, much more when over Pressured.

He started sobbing all throughout his life at an end. "I can't fail my family".

Continuing.

"Look..., *I want his body*' !!

At that, A creature said again revealing itself blue with its arms crossed standing familiar to what was accustomed of visitations prier.

The boy starts to faint.

"ONE OF US!!"

An alien gray appears in a form of enhanced CGI. Flying as if to show off in a rapid pace of action.

A Light show of occultist expression. The boy still holding on to dear life. Remaining in the chair.

Next a character appears displaying in a form of an avatar, like with an entourage as they called out **"Toonami"**! Deceptively present with characteristics known from a familiar earthly source, *Count Dooku*, played by *Christopher Lee*. From *Star Wars* revamps of the early 2000s. As unusual as it was, others in this insanity appeared in front of him to display as a selected character unformulated but a presence of them not to be taken lightly.

A black character came in next. It wasn't of human identity.

It's alias being called as the *ultimate evil*. It was then a third mysterious figure. Of Unknown came forward too, aligned with the others facing one another. It was that where the host drifted closer to a rest.

Screen changes, **Toonami** displaying itself now as a presence of source and power. Opening an illusion of doors and lines of circles from behind this character resembling other planets.

"PROFECIA!, PROFECIA!" says the entourage of Grey aliens behind more extravagant members.

Dazed and puzzled it was the last thoughts. Only for those doors to remain open and his mind lost in an anguish as to "how in the *fuck*" does this happen to him along a *background* with amazement as a cherry on top. Faints. Pain, disappearing that instant.

Strangest behavior, with so many different outcomes of unusual perversions every character now dispersed.

Nothing could account for betrayal this young man felt. How a year post of this accident in a building called Guilford County Behavioral Health Center. Where being rushed from an ambulance could for tell.

"GOD USE ME, to clean the world with waters"

"Grant me the voice and wisdom of *Solomon the Great*" "To aid the people and heal the nations with my voice"

Now the world was darker and his eyes remained closed a year hence that prayer. How things could fall to such lows of existence to murder and mayhem, mind control of children as a barbaric advantage. Further then the Earths Achievements in science and technology. Has this come to a horrid surprise.

There was *pity*, only *pity* noticed and felt.

CHAPTER XII
"GOD OF PITY"

"What the hell" "Where am I?"

"I can't believe it, I'm alive..."

"This mattress is hard and my back hurts" "What time is it"?

"TAP-TAP" *KNOCKS ON THE DOOR*

"Yes"?

"Lunch is ready"! "Lunch"?

"I guess that answers my question" "*GRRRRRP!*"

"Stomachs hurting, and I'm starving now that she mentioned it." "How did I get into these cloths"

"What am I doing here?, How am I going to get out of this"?

Had it been the clothes he was wearing resembling pajamas to leave the impression he had gone MAD. Such would be the embarrassment of his family to see him in such situation. That alone would've costed a fortune to repair his personal credit and hospital bill. Time would continue to favor the odds against it.

As detailed, like a baby first using its eyes, there being unease out of what happened to our young host the other day. Left dazed, weakened and surprisingly alive. So much has happened over the span of a year from since these entities first started communicating with him. Far from broken, Picking his legs up, walking jaded of entertainment. straight for the front desk. "Excuse me!, I'd like to know If I can leave soon, I have work to get to." Referencing his job as a waiter, wishful his head straighten better. Unfortunately ironic he ends up in a mental hospital.

"There's just no way to know right now, You'll have to wait for the doctor to give you that answer I am afraid" says the attendant. "Damn", boy looking down resentfully, patient is the patient.

Walking away he hears a calling for others to line up going forth to the cafeteria. Behind a line of fools and helpless, left inside a mental hospital. Isolated, Not a soul dared to stare. There wasn't time to befriend anyone. Wearing socks in a line dragging dirt, restricted of wearing shoes or sandals. When it was time to eat there was a tray of food you took back to your room and ate there.

No access to cellular device or belongings. Not even a television. You needed permission to access the only wired phone on a wall. A gentle smile seeing a nugget, His Journal was still near. Notes held close to his body unbelievable. kept him alive and more then content. It all showed a very clear message. Whatever he had, whatever happened to him. What was going on now. Had to be very important for others to know of. There we're things here on this planet that wanted little of progress made of his efforts to convince people of being under aggressive supervision.

It came as God, all loving and generous of time. Now it's displaying itself as irrational. Clear indications suggested it to be concrete evidence of extraterrestrials. They are sending out a message that is perverted and disgraceful in context to a plan. A plan it wanted to linger above our atmosphere eating out of our cerebral cortex. Without regard to our laws or moral integrity.

Military's made deals with these hostilities and whatever the case was. Both presents to the young man had to be controlled by some third party of sorts. So without disregard, knowing it had to be a difficulty to move this message of understanding to the masses would have a consequence of retaliation from these deranged lunatics. Chasing and plotting to play murder.

"I guess that's why these things we're always remaining hidden", "they didn't want to be bothered from people knowing how their eating out of us." Boy, now in a mental recovery.

"KNOCKS ON THE DOOR."

"There's a phone call for you" a nurse says. "I'll be there in a minute!", Thanks!

Rushing out of bed and into the hallways moving his food tray. He picks up his confidence and speaks "hello".

"HEY, WHERE ARE YOU?!!?"

"How did you know where to find me?" "I thought you left"..Young Man responds to not only but his heroin, who must've disparately tried locating him. "I'm sick and worried about you!","I'm driving to come visit and pick you up! and make sure you're doing OK." "You're mom is worried sick of you too".

After hearing from her feeling his heart drops. Realizing how lucky he is to being in love with such a beautiful great girl. She loved him dearly and finding the young man's wear a bout's showed clearly she stood as his rock. His pillar of comfort and strength. "Fuck me".

"If a million loved you, I am one of them. If one loved you, it was me. If no one loves you know that I am dead". ~Franz Kafka

Six days went by. Eagerly he couldn't wait to get out of it.

Finally being able to see the sun. Hopeful for the best. Knowing those things never left. Knowing they would return and more than likely throw more A.I computerized cartoons in his head. What's the point of the sharp drilling pain they forced in his brain was, had no definite answer either. "No problem! although when I do get out, I'm gonna tell everyone, I know about what's really going on with me..

It bothers the hell out of me how naive these things had me running around the grocery store!, Calling my mother?!, "PITIFUL!" "ONE OF US"?! Recalling that thing preaching. A gray alien. It's what ran in the young man's head those nights, Restlessness was a gift. Fucking creature was an outer space monster on drugs no doubt about it. Who knows if it was still screeching its heart out.

Absorbing our kind as source.

Eager the day he left, sweet heart outside waiting. A different God came to focus without denial of other existence. Driving away, his lady curious and meaning to know what his story was. "There's a God! I'm alive". Looking at the sky as he sat in the passenger seat of the vehicle. Day bright, warm weather, Summer time hitting his smile. Mouth open of conversations chattering to her, not being able to recall. Though the good comfort in being able to speak to some-one, while muted those days. Keeping to himself. You could imagine the outspoken words filled with odd brilliance. On the other hand.. *Doctors noted him a Schizophrenic.*

More time went by and the host now the bold "God of Pity".

Ever so squinting of the gaze given of what was, has and is to be. Felling discomfort being the only real deity in a new life of struggle against the dark. A pursuit of peace, now had information given by bits. Much of the material was consistency pressured onto him to listen. Everywhere he went. While working being with consistent like personal life meant on it. "One of us" was a promise.

They wanted to be a part of his life and time. Distaste in the knowl-edge and wisdom God poured onto him so foolishly.

Receiving information was all due to the exact telling of earlier constructs between the worldly to share upon. Had there be the skill of precaution to hold back the urge to yell. God Forbid a Hypocritical Golden boy packed of confidence would be the voice of the people.

Governments, military, Corporate and occult's to market independent human life as well sexuality to extraterrestrials in exchange for other notes and blueprints. It had clearly gone haywire with blackmail pouring to a kid telekinetic-ally communicated into his brain by satellite. Sounded like work of science fiction but other technologies we're being involved in this struggle and who knew how many others around the world being forced into this scheme. The amount of Manpower to orchestrated such instances claimed indications to be of hundreds to thousands.

Starting to notice his surroundings changing, cartoons and animations of creatures playing inside his mind start to go buzzing around his head. Resemblance to imaginary friends, these friendly woodland critters would not be trusted. There was need to find professionalism in this situation yet, they had been vulgar and grotesque. Chasing him around in a form queer, the halls as he walked calmly battered, they still riddling about what to do with him next.

Having to dress himself at times and halt time with his own privately. It was a disaster. He loved himself and who he was with. A sudden understanding of what was around him grew obviousness that of being favorite, to what was engaged into looking out the eyes of HIS BODY. This was heavily monitored.

There was no denial now receiving sexual harassment. From various voices. Including a line of apparent Government tools and assets ranging from every Department in the Country.

Debilitating further action in a day's routine. Never alone, structure was starting to tighten his rooms. His own doors locked him out of air. Feeling confined to stay Drift, championing his day. Like no other! Imbeciles! He'd tell them! "The Day is mine" was at an ease of winners! But what was his weakness, was the thought of her being targeted. It was of luck to be accustomed to loneliness. Thing about that, it's also a weapon capable of harming or strength building as an apprehensive man would think.

A new day set itself upon the boy. As he got up from bed living as a modern day hustling aristocrat. Opening Curtains in his room, followed with skips to the bathroom preparing himself.

Looking at the mirror was the shock that defined further obviousness to what he already knew. Something else was staring back.

"He looks good today"..

Said a soft voice in his head persuading that there was an other perspective having conversations of him. As if to feel frowned upon, it was the bitch of people in the pentagon setting him up. An obvious choice of poor dialog to bring down a gentlemen with willpower and integrity shamelessly. All to protect their own asses and assemblies.

"WE NEED TO SILENCE YOUR VOICE"

What was this enemy, to which was the challenge he'd receive. Had it been from Creator himself to counter such. In contrary it was highly necessary to bestow as much of his personal keys of knowledge to as much of another presence as a defensive. There was a voice in his head that would reply through these dumbfounded surveillance programs. It was critical of his personal safety to remain calm. Being in the heat of opposition.

Consequently, these groups stretched around the land would not jeopardize its history in the modern world.

As a supreme dominance to whatever society brought up.

Those that knew played puzzled. Comforted in a bubble of sorts. They wanted more of it and gathered like crowds to watch his life from inside another body. Eating. touching, watching and knowing of him or his loved ones naked together. Uncomfortable was as precise to point what flaws there are in the room with him. Had it all Struck his mind and thinking.

"Go fuck yourself" the host would toss to "it" brushing his teeth in front of the mirror. Profoundness of his bloodlines blessing of handsomeness was enough motivation. He now knew the devils lair and it was his head. Looking straight without breaking a sweat. *"What would anyone now do about this situation"* was now a new found response of push. Cunning would be a define maneuver of style in the way you fling insults. It was consistent as the clock on a watch.

Time measured the globe around, hurrying to work was the key to existing, It was always against him knowing what opponent would try to both censor and aggravate the kid. Knowing Meditation as you walk and having your mind blank as the thing whispered had been the perfect opportunity to engage wit. Thus was wit on his side when work would question his abilities but remaining strong in the fires of hell is life. Shrugging and doing for years. Time at his side but it would only prove again and again to be here limited.

As the day drew closer to noon. Being definite need to open publicly, what would intelligence be if not passed on to another, Does it not halt it? There was necessity to progress in what now was a personal investigation towards stopping persistent threats he, receiving. It meant action! Persistence in resources. Eyeing police, fire department, Calling straight forward ALL DEPARTMENTS in the Country. It at times rejected even met with occasional backlash.

For that example it didn't matter. Point is in any situation to spread what you got like water, *spray lightly* without drenching the cloth in front of you. Make sure it's simple to uplift and control the liquid. It wasn't just about verbal dialects. It was also a sell. "How can I get people to buy into the fact that my life is in jeopardy because of the knowledge of what's out here, aliens are real, and I know what they're doing and the governments associates with them as well".

Gucci glasses on his face and dirt thrown at a man's character. Like the saying goes, "There is a time and place for everything". Wearing a shirt and tie, correcting his image. It didn't matter. Proper direction in pace with rhythm being a benefit of upbeat to what was told to everybody around his presence. Guy had a taste for independent artists. Keeping music, pinnacle of that which is remedy for staying afloat and empowered.

Key Ethos, How to inform others included selling what was important. Pathos in acknowledging how others would entertain the idea of being watched and monitored by weaponized space technologies found a flout in all surrounding space. Lagos was the need for more evidence to distribute such claims. Then an execution of Kairos, final strategy, move at the right time at any given. This being the formula. Blessings had it for one to move on their own. A small stone had changed form.

CHAPTER XIII
"KAIROS"

"So we danced with a rifle, to the rhythm of the gun in a
glade through the trees I saw my only one"
"Then the Earth seemed to rise hell hot as the sun" "The
soldiers were dying, there was tune to the sighing."
"The Song was an old Rebel One"

~ Rebel Waltz, The Clash.

Videos were independently made and adjusted in continuation to how useful it would prove for someone. Obviousness that where there is need, action must follow. Some cardboard was bought white and colored with markers for the words to stand out. A selection of different communications with various groups was a considerable approach. There was limited resources regardless the point being how to get this docile movement of an inhabitant away from his presence. They weren't taken lightly but considerable insults consistently said towards them seemed to encourage more motive to ruin one another. This presence of insect in various forms was both cunning and rapid in offensive as progression pushed the blade.

A private meeting with a pastor took hold in those days to show some concrete material. Including pictured documentations of entities on his parents' property. From precursor exposure, It was a sight for those able to pick up outlines in the print.

Notebooks of conversations included written down for some time now. Promised by his own progression. "One of us", still present in the confused standard how open they deemed him of worth in such a strange ritual as from the start to the visit to a mental rehabilitation building. Yet in a church, Preacher David was open to listen.

"Hola, pastor!"

"Estoy presentado a ti en admiration, en la vida ay cosas bien uniqas. Donde depas todo, uno tiene que platecar de importancia de informationes para los demas."

"I'm being followed and stalked by something, I believe the United States Government has something to do with it."

"I have evidence to suggest it's also in collaboration with other things".

"To what extent are you referring to?" says the preacher. *"What do you think of Extraterrestrials?"*

Timed at an hour. Some facts on how these entities handled themselves towards a young adult had grave information of these malicious groups around the world and other, thriving inside our bodies cybernetic-ally. It plagued relationships and humble people that devoted their lives worshiping familiar religion. It was cataloged to suggest some details of mass murder and mayhem to innocence.

For a reason of some ill minded distaste of entertainment. It ruined lives. Knowing of the presence was suggested a curse from other things. With that, was no suitable means to further activity with it at the cost of safety. All throughout being that enough meant lives and loved ones potentially attacked. There was necessary action.

"I was forced to see and hear things attacking me daily, molesting my family and attempting to murder those around me. No solutions but to let everyone know, yet when I spoke back to these things humbly and patiently to be left alone. Voices of officials and madmen we're wasteful and disgusting towards my consistent work and pace of how I handled my things."

Pastor David wasn't able to grasp these things as evidence was passed and so were the notes. He took an eye at the photographs present at the time. These items weren't tampered with. Plenty of details that did become open to his ears had dark tones and ill said issues of the sinister evils in society. Much was said and as quick as time flew.

The conversation and interests to continue we're present and done. It was hard to listen and know of many of those details in person. Much more, present speech in a church of Government and Extraterrestrial movements as a crisis to a man who knew only of God gave it more chills in a meeting of the two.

Young man packs his work, there being one thing. Leaving the preacher with none other than entrusted with two notebooks of writing involving some evidence of recorded conversations written down. No other way around, "If something we're to happen to me, says the young researcher. Keep them as proof of what's happen. It's very important I leave them in the hands of someone I can trust in any case for this matter. God Forbid."

Chasing, quickly maneuvering thoughts. It was of keen interests to get out of it! Pushing the gas while keeping it at speed limit when on the road heading downtown. "You weren't suppose to know so much information. We told you plenty of times we would find use for you". "Go fuck yourself" he replies. Finally drawing closer to a near by parking deck building.

Idea was that if it is in a satellite. The concrete in the lowest levels would sure do the trick and losing these guys. With a brush of resistance he drives right in. Did it work?, Sure didn't. It sank.

The agony of how does one live his life with such disfiguring of issues from a higher ground of a masochistic evil.

"Doesn't work, just so you know." Says cunningly a hunter in his head. "You have to do everything we ask you to do", "As well allow us access to your body willingly". "IF YOU DON'T MOVE WE WILL FIRE YOU"... At some effort of claims to move direct attacks on a victim, had broken stability further in this situation. It was of adequate need to survive anything coming, preparation had not been at the side.

Smacking his lips, young man grabs some material in his Ford he left inside. Rolls in the back seat grasping aluminum foil. Heavy amounts had apparent attributes to reflect signals and radio frequencies. Grabbing black tape wrapping those layers together. One end to the other in the form of a helmet and body armor, covering everything. It seemed difficult for these entities to reach full extent of power. After his own examinations it was clear.

Control of sound on a point of interest being his brain was none other than entering into the openings of his ears and head.

These signals we're bouncing from the bottom up. How they did it was a feat very pest. It must've taken mad science to utilize such monstrous tactics. Making his way to the bottom of some stairs, holding dear to his material. They were on his back, the noises would not cease. Much less now, notice formulated pack the United States military and its branches along with a long list of legislators now entwined with the aliens had taken part in this.

Patiently waiting for cease of waterboarding attacks needy of moving lowest. Having the strength of Hercules was idea when confronting such rare circumstances. No telling how many would come his way asking questions now that he's made more public openings of his work and research as well along the shear disrupting behaviors of many others towards us. During timing of more open approach of extraterrestrials causing global media to respond to Pentagon reports.

It was obviousness that surges of interests for these things being all over the place. In that statement news broke of speeds exceeding standard performance of most aircraft even more modernized equipment from China barely came par of what documentations reported. No one wanted his information to be everywhere, yet having control of the host was a scheming priority. Continuing to sit and remain calm as he gathered thoughts.

Getting back up and rushing back to his vehicle, roams back home. The devils followed realizing the world now changing.

It was top grade stuff, There was no chance we would have a hand at this. Processing what was being generated claimed a downfall to

Earths humanity if in the case of war with this. There was too much to lose, strategies without hurting the public just couldn't be aligned with what the Government wanted. Martial law, full powers to certain separation of powers. It would prove such an issue to American flexibility of freedoms.

Its where these desires eroded from at a base root of a congressman's skull. What sense of persuasions had there been in a table of men who spoke of such. An agenda for Martial law? Unless it was declared that they too wanted knowledge and use from these entities as much as the rich and needy, they having interaction with aliens. It was no wonder being selected and present could be identified as warmongering with persistence to edge on throats.

With too many with an out of jail free card. It's deceptive when a standard policy would otherwise say no and move objective to deny these people any further powers to preserve them. Excuses such as "What would the media say?" "This department would be under fire". "Don't cross the line". Being part of the deal would be human utilization of extraterrestrials and their ships techniques in exchange for it all being in the dark.

Simple white supremacy dominating the intelligence of their owns people. Even influencing segregation and sales of who's a better man based off the body. Distasteful and small. Such beauty in the people for actions to disrupt society in pain. Hiding the total effects of their wording and mental state to a population of more intelligence. Simply by the succumbed mind of another who puts effort into polishing them. It was this group of people that monitored with the aliens and indulged together as long as they kept one another going with whatever is that they wanted. Being in the form of a pact, proving interests in science to stay on top pressuring hysteria.

Generals, Colonels, Commanders in the United States so caught up in an eating disorder with aliens. So many excuses. A pain to see so many interesting people suffering saying no word to other senators or personal after the baby boomer generation.

Generations that followed, Of a more feeble and unacknowledged base in root. Thus a dramatic shift in new information circulating the cold back of Western Countries maneuverability in these frontiers of space. With limited movement and those with information grilled as conspiracy theorists.

No wonder no one spoke of these happenings. A menagerie in tune as a cage to imprison. Feeding and looking at such gullible evolution. Laughable Capricho. "At least he didn't starve" being of ill intent. With steady notes, much of illustrations that did make it to the young man's collection. In which in part was growing high when staked. There was hunger to ease off the writing.

Knowing very well that that too could be the reason these entities would speak on the behalf of what then was captured in details. So much for fruits of knowledge. Carnage far from absent filled the stomach of meat. It was names of bodies of cataclysm from the results of these entities that kept the writer at bay.

Knowing very well with that information and those puzzles of the world in possession.

A mind was always full, heavy and of loss of concentrations from what would've been a normal functioning life. A sense of mentorship was present. Rare circumstances of it. With that he so "Didn't Starve", Gluttony was present in the world of politics and self enrichment seekers.

It's the irritating behavior of how unmotivated some of the lessons and plots from both sides now pursuing the young man and the information they could milk from him. All while deforming his uniqueness and further cry of technologies in space to present themselves in his home to torture.

His writings and conversations with the Dark, seemed to encourage unwanted attentions daily. Base root to becoming from elsewhere away from home or any locations of presence through the day. Being near absolute of a theory proven. It is Satellites and other worldly craft observing with schemes to engage he who knew now more then enough. Out in the distance the East had made headlines.

China was at the doorsteps with other nations and American men in all departments allowed this. Each pointing the finger at the other. As the list grew so did wisdom of personal judgment. Clear in the middle of fire, Such hostility was meant as personal attacks to the boy and those around in presence. It ended up with calls to others domestically as well as around the world. To notice.

In those hours of the time. Came along gaps of resistance consistently. Barbaric threats and mind altering attacks with sounds and screeches, There was no cease, neither was the boy stopping. Years would stretch, It was a blend of order and stupendous chaos. Irony being that order was present itself to be at most part of percentage from the writer himself. A speaker was necessary, thus the need to move at accuracy. Only problem, "How to acquire more additional proof?!"

"You need to go to the capital and speak of it" would say some of these other worldly entities. It was difficult to say who it was now showing themselves to be huddled in those crafts at times like back doors the military would offer them. "Why would you tell me this? Kid had it hard, his permits to stay in the country under DACA had been sabotaged so had his labor. Its part of the market the boy would speak to himself to progress answers from that which was present at the time. "We've seen this before"!, "It was an offer from the market John offered". "Whose John"?. "Its what everyone around the world calls the United States military and its department staff as well as others in the country that know of these matters."

It wasn't clear if "John" was an actual person but an alias to which extent was presumed was accurately depicted as that.

Regardless the circumstances being present that even after efforts of callings directly and having others know of these happenings couldn't be enough to help others be alerted. Alerting others without causing them to look at you as a disabled being. Being difficult to convince the community in the field with features to state the reality of issues in him personally and other wise them.

These entities, this "John" and everyone else all intertwined in a spectacle of pushing and pulling. It was always a force of kinetic energy that held these people imprisoned with the son of a bitch.

No one seemed to want to leave the young man alone or get out. Yet infrequency there being a second of peace and no one bothering self–benevolence.

"They must've left the room".. "Where ever they would be sitting and talking off on a mic" It's obvious these guys we're terrified of exposure to the public. Including the Extraterrestrials, How pleasant of them to leave him daily with huge amounts of information and draw of attentions from others. Just bringing it all to another doorsteps.

No matter the case, books in possession was a baby. Held tight and at an eye with clumsy need to leave it stranded somewhere, sometimes. Right then and there it was picked back up, reread and drawing attention again. Just to look at these books now time had aged it, becoming "MYTHICAL CURSED GOLD".

CHAPTER XIV
"MYTHICAL CURSED GOLD!"

Mercury – "!!So slippery it will fall from your skin!!" Atomic Number – 80
Symbol – Hg "Poisonous Quicksilver"

A Brain has natural elements of different and unique metals, copper, gold even iron traced inside the human body. Necessary as bodies nutrient yet potentially cause harm if a certain limit is reached. Your brain a treasure chest, from millions of years of evolution. Copper, magnesium and many others. Microscopic, yet many studies have concluded they reside in there. How that came to be theoretically, from openings of our heads. Being a door to little other things, to enter and rest somewhere in the matter of our wonderful self conscious. Sometimes we can hear sounds unfamiliar enter as well. Such as that *consistent weeping of voices that now more present then ever in a hosts membrane.*

If it weren't for music and laughter that now present in the rituals of what surrounded the young inhabitant of Greensboro, North Carolina. Irony, war chants and tears from acute disorientation. Undeniable of attention to be looked at. It was now a battle of the day. Resistance to hold back from familiars that grew along. It was a disturbing case of loneliness and need. "Who the hell could possibly be involved in this too". "There's no way I'm the only one."

A count in crisis of how many illustrated documents now in multitudes exceeding his personal wants or expectations. You could say it was a mindset of wanderlust rather than proud and realization of the new found collection of notes now stacked. Much depicting manners of potential room for science and law. There was a libretto in the pages and it told time.

Past, Present and Future. Events dating of conversations that would continue from the base of current happenings. To modernized potential of human ingenuity and rights. There was no peace without resistance, being present. Boxing in the dark with things unnoticeable yet persistent. Counterattacks of deep space entities and their defenses as well as offenses disabling many manners of natural flow in the day. It had been cataloged and implemented shadowed by panic and haste.

Clear in situations where these defenses originated from, outer space encounters to military alliances nesting together. It was all military, to which they encouraged fear and physical to mental obstructions on the young host. A man with knowledge had been a direct threat to a market after all. There was no telling how much of Government and affiliates had been programmed and misdirected in all ways further alienating themselves and the people.

All seemed to come forth with a different mindset then other functional inhabitants. More aggressive and showing poor strategy. Much being an embarrassment of action on how to handle these sort of situations. Why there was a unity, had been questioned.

They all wanted something from the other and the young man was shown "it" in third perspective. As back as it could get. It was resting in our heads, something had entered to show forth evidence to support so many claims.

How could he show that evidence to anyone being near of an impossible feat. There was just no way to inform others of these doings without there being recordings of what was shown in his mind. So the only clear method in this place of action was to write it all down. Writing vasts notes into books would win. It always has, someone would pick information up like a sponge. Test his own intelligence and sophistication. Followed by educating deeper into further details of the phenomenon as mush of studies into the dark.

Someone or Something regardless had the powers to move people to the most high of conscious and understanding technologically. Had it been the young man himself to witness and judge man for his sins and gain roots of knowledge from now a more advance reason to which he was implemented to see. It was prescribed to him to take medication and he maintained powers of ancestral glory as a member of eternal. Looking at the walls in tirelessness. In that instant of peace he knew the difficulty it would be to remain structured without misdirecting others.

Being in the background had been him as a character. Given an option to speak of what was happening around us. Yet was continually assaulted and pushed further in a different world of rule that was enacting on human Earthly society. It had not been Gods answer but was welcomed like it without another option to take the place. To document Dark. men, women and children being sold for sexual labor and entertainment for fetish driven needs of outer space aliens. While military and world corporate men who knew and served to these things that took one side. A point in which the United States military along with Soviet Union and other malicious white extremists controlled a world wide sex ring. Filled with drugs and kidnappings.

Drunk with borrowed money which was both stolen and lied about as a "means for study". Meanwhile, in real time E. Ts shown exercises of a hole in Antarctica's atmosphere. A familiar face of "trust wordy human alliances",as a case and reminder of duties to protect civilizations from near damnation. Had been what kept him alive all those years. Showed the boy how it was being closed. A reactor in the middle of the Arctic being utilized as "Plasma energy" as they called it. Disabled and blown to bits. Being modified and controlled by hazard genius mad scientists both World wide organizations like NATO having presence. Spliced Homunculus beings shown as two of them, repairing and taking maintenance of these reactors while they being monitored by men in suits.

They we're building boogeymen shit underground. Like a VILLAINS secret lair. Right before the events of it being shut down. Acknowledgment how dangerous and end of world tampering some of these things from outer space really are. They wanted to kill humans.. It was in the need to see us tremble. Thus on the year of 2021 news broke of the Antarctic Hole closing up over its hemisphere. Hopeful the world would heal, our host was selected to witness this.

Secret Warmongering on the day, being taught how to take advantage but the boy knew better. Yet it would be recognized that this knowledge would not go without its downfall of agony. He was already being forced in a form of a cover up story. Being limited of what could be spoken out aloud, the Government itself pissed itself knowing that there was a guy out loose knowing everything.

Cunning and of ill mind, had it been given to implement as he dared and wanted to. Thus enemies had rose from it, What to do with this.

Those things had been drooling, mass scouts of them on the moon. Just staring at us with an erection. Preying on civilians.

They couldn't get enough of sexual desires. Thus the noticeable drive to maintain a world wide movement to give them whatever they wanted. Nuking the moon in secret, What to do in the mean time? Give them the people, In exchange for disruptive human life as a totality.

Promises of eternal life in an elixir and a move to deep sleep while "day walking in a hibernation chamber". Where the flesh levitated in water, Breathing and thriving just like the aliens inside of our bodies. Near Invisible, over our attic. Painful to see these catalogs of information in the form of shows in your head. There being present things devouring our time having made man mad.

It was crucial for a movement to cease these conversations and neutral needs of writing texts. Being moved from different identities to disable personality. It was happening while the young man given these articulate details to document while it would last. Thinking was how these scumbags walked on Earth. Agencies of the present time around the world knew very well he was being "studied and checked" with as well taught of how *Gods of Destruction* played on our world. Reality, there was not one species of alien but several hundred to thousands. A communications ring, placed from a space guild of intelligence to a slave market monitored by its own style of militarism.

Money spent to just be evil and do evil things. A grown man should've known right from wrong, at least know when to cease such behavior. As it was sorted there was indications of something leeched onto them. There was a bigger alien in the background. It was hungry, needy and unflattering of itself. Many victims and professionals came in unity to talk of these forwarded investigations.

Unfortunately it was all the same thing, whatever was keeping him alive was eating out of him and his life as much as the enemy. Would that not have stated to be the culprit of who was haunting us? Multiple sides had been in the field after all including thieves and liars of liberty and order. There have been claims some private alliances tugging and moving the doomsday clock. End-of-World theorists having been a problem. Many of which without knowing of what they do. We all we're being watched including whatever flocks had been lingering around good and bad of a cause.

Primordial Powers that remained hidden and stalking the lands of its people with personal wars.

Just as hungry and reckless. War mongering and famine onto Terra's civilizations, with a different side of things. Came to be people like ours. In which formulated a plan to save the world and others around. A call in a sort to know when to strike against old age pests. They assembled and gathered just as infiltrated space technologies to free the people that we're once caught in a web of lies.

These UFOS were hubs to which they also met and checked who was around the perimeter and sectors of space. At that, how the sense of battle with spirit was endless. Yet there was the question if that too was a sale. To keep the young man at bay with rhythms of survival feeling empathy and remorse of his breathe and the hands that made him. Seeing many people die because of space and its bullshit. It was his mother's prayer heard that he was still alive. "He's still alive?!?"

It struck something to see a man fight and struggle with his day as intelligent as he was because of being neat of a person. Knowing good from evil and calling out for aid. Thus assembles of others showed presence from experience at dealing with monsters and their behavior. So it was bought up by so many. So many people would go to these new idols and heroin from outer space.

Including the Army, everyone needed answers and when some got it. They didn't like it and went after those that "knew too much".

Private investigations came silent as everyone else that first stranded themselves in as guys room. Some rookies more than likely that weren't clearly told of full disclosure. Such difficulty of a mess to know that the world needed open talks on all this. They just wanted the young man out of it. It made everyone nervous.

How a man danced on the top, watching everything consumed with a straw. This top of the pyramid scheme, order of occult's and sacred power was non other than extraterrestrials playing with everyone's head using technology.

Sweating those hands prune. No one wanted prosecutions that they would face now that the message was gaining attention. It wasn't enough to see some investigators led astray from their departments strategists. Whereabouts and proper ways to capture these events in a place like the hosts had remained disclosed. Al because of so much

'White Nationalism' lost in Wisdom the entities proved to be very crafty and mischievous.

Masterminds after all was of them coming from eons of self destruction and sabotage, they didn't just take control of your ears they enslaved them. Whip Masters of a White Slave, Alien Gods of an ironic surrealist picture. They used computers, massive amounts of them too. Planetary in scale and whatever else potentially orbiting their homeland. Must've taken hundreds of thousands of years for their primitive stages to manufacture them since the creation of their first computers and semi-conductors. Everybody that studied these fought for a share of knowledge.

No one wanted to lose power. They all sold it differently and occasionally had their share of rape onto man using re-engineered space alien machinery "that we call satellites" . Harsh in an environment and unnecessary entitlement to those that abused it. Unwelcoming of a dilemma for an entire assembly of men and women uneducated or ill informed of the United States military's behaviors behind closed doors. Absence of strategy or protective enactments. More so a gathering of wants and needs. Where all being very observed in a collective hivemind with extraterrestrials and other foreigners spelling doom.

A hive mind being present and active in the nation. Everyone was forced into a new brink of front line diseases following rapid responses, to medical cures coming from over the counter lined for those "First Come, First Serve" routines from the enacted fear the media would portray. Its origins of COVID as example always a mystery from the ground up there was rumors of it potentially escaping a lab. Even a purposely used bio weapon of its own, directed at everyone especially the inhabitants of the United States.

After months of extensive need to contain such things, It was always multiplying and mutating into different strands. In efforts hundreds of thousands to millions suffering even fallen to the new plague which where ever it rose from. "It was created by us and experimented in a space station." Says one of thee hosts entities passing on this sort of information. Which over time had grown to be more ludicrous and entertained in knowing all.

It was then a revelation opened taking hold of everyone's observations in dread of light. Of it all being a set up and a game of its own from outer space intruders. Mad men from around the world and clan devoted enriched. Neo-Malthusian ideology found COVID led as an example. As well as its cure. It was another plan to control the world's population. A true card of soul monopoly, true reason,

TO DELIEVER METALS INTO THE HUMAN BODY BY THE VACCINES (MERCURY, INFILTRATED TO REACT THE MEDICINE), DIGESTED, MOVED USING RADAR INSTRUMENTS WHILE STATIONARY IN OUR BEDS, FROM "OTHERS" SUB ATOMICALLY DELIEVERING THESE METALS SURGICALLY TO THE HUMAN CEREBULLUM AND PLANTED AS FORCED BRAIN IMPLANTS, CONTROLLING US.

Excruciating of a reality, while everyone in America was placed in an artificial bubble. Using satellites to move particles found in the body and collect them in a single point to track you, monitor your brain as well as control it with direct programming meant a scene of downfall for mankind. These entities hacked the antennas on our sophisticated instruments and even potential to send out mass programming onto the public. Having it all been interlinked.

It would've meant lawsuits, exterminations of these traitors and end of the need to upkeep that which motivated these patterns since early stages. Put simply those surrounding the young man, Fear mongering lunatics with powers that unseen to others in blinds view. This was out there playing with us to all who prayed for savior in America. Everything was funded there was no excuse not to move on this more effectively. Parasites had evolved with wings and they took control.

Veterans asking for money, that's who was sitting in the biggest chairs in the pentagon. They being responsible yet neglectful at the damage circulating. Obviousness they knew what was going on, drunkenness no responsibilities being truly enacted. All those that opposed would inevitably vanish or go disorientated. It was too late for some, there was just no way "John" wanted to lose his power over men and women he'd fuck over. It made women horny as hell with aliens involved manipulating them for one another. Had it been the plot "to taste" together anyway.

That alone being enough for Naval officers and commands to follow a guide line of not shooting these hazards or moving aggressively against their own faults. Caught in a labyrinth with the devil was long term life style being happy to oblige to. Military turned fake pimps. CIA and FBI having knowledge with other departments wanting a share of these powers and how to sexually control women and young girls into sleeping with them.

With an addition to microchip production and modern day mans needs for further sale of an update, a brain implant was highly sought after for entertainment and control of the human conscious. Internet access and linked to a space satellite would offer a new look onward. Proving only to mislead and malformed man like bugs collecting information for the Hive. They would thrive in our bodies. Space dilemma of how to get to the other planet was met with conscious hopping onto a human host or other. Without the need of traveling to a new terrain or planet.

This science was already proven a failure, a disgrace.

All we're being marketed, many men like minded and ours came forth with the pledge to protect the people had gone the other way. Direction to aid innocence pacing towards a path where information as such would be shared, reminded with grace of how we mustn't stray away from our humble beginnings. Makeshift plans for peace with the string pullers.

There was war all over the place because of communications that derived from radar added radio. Once one got interested to communicating with the other. Hostility would prove to be present provocations of facts that lump sums went to the wrong hands being paid for need to create disasters for our general public. Even while paying a share of taxes was the average man met in life being fed to monsters from outer space in privacy.

At addition of nannite brain adjusted technologies onto our Grey/white matters met with conflicts. Just a need for it presented persistence of something other then human, wanting a "taste".

Some dark hidden science would prove that physical metals inside the body would expose a host to entities. Advance systems would pinpoint and stalk civilians who uneducated, would have trace of such in their bodies. Beautiful people being highly sought after as much because of what we carried in our pockets, a cellphone.

Everyone needed a step up from this and luckily there being certain protections who disastrously also abused what was entrusted. There was a problem. Our eyes in the skies welcomed the idea of beings called Gods. Ferociously abused their powers and those accounted for judged. Sucked out those blamed, like a straw as witnesses presented. All due respect, it was a lot of information that would have been difficult to peace together properly. Being upfront even the young man would suffer for what was passed directly at him, while being harassed and hazed by humans playing with satellites.

How dishonorable for people in our homeland to claim as of virtuous principles.

It would prove to mentor others more peacefully then recklessness portrayed by such disgusting behavior. American Military wanted none of it. They wanted this hidden and left out while they continued playing a game of who sits as *god and pawn today.* It was serious and there being no results to educate the public. Driven mad, These entities controlled their minds and direction on what procedures would better "Preserve Peace and Prosperity in the Nation" Aliens wanted full control of everything.

When investigation had led onto what the Young man was undergoing. Proving more difficult of a challenge to control the problem that would follow him at home. When the rest of the Government found out, they had been told to keep it secret and walk away from it. No matter the case the young man had his notebooks and spent his nights after work writing all he was told and held cybernetic witness of.

Everyone was being led on and lied to. It was met with backlash the young man now attacked with further pain and blackmail. Crushing his heart out of hopes for aid. Old men in space hated his youth and educated intelligence of preservation. It was such a problem for the truth to be spoken and laughably by the day there was notice of arrests and eliminations of nationalist and alien pacts falling from power. Only problem was the department took its time and would steal credit of all front lines as presumed. Being, men and women from other places not of this planet and a hand full of others including the young man himself.

For now there had been a present battle hidden gloriously. In other places the military was hiding all its gold and fancy jewels it stole and looked at all day. While offering human flesh like as prostitutes with sex machines they planted to be of use. Controlled by the entities themselves. It proved how further disregarded of ethnics, whom was in power spent money. It proved how much of a failure would be opened up of similar stories that surrounded these now more detailed occultists in Uniform, Suits and Robes practiced with their friends from space.

CHAPTER XV
"FRIENDS FROM SPACE"..

!!Caution Beware!!: Of

TOXIC PEDIOPHILIAC HOMOSEXUAL NIGHTCRAWLING

NECROPHILIAC ZOMBIE CANNIBAL ROBOT

ANIMILPHILIAC

SEXUAL PREDATOR MONSTERS FROM OUTERSPACE

!!THEY MAY BE RADIOACTIVE!!

In all there's something to admire about the now contagious setting these beings evoked. There was persistence and tactical abuse being spread openly all over those overseeing. Those being in direct contact with the young host who determined with concentration lined details of what was and what has happened in events accordingly. Humorous, they say the quickest way to a women's heart is to keep her laughing. Being clingy and at some form protective of how the cataclysmal in essence, threw a guy in the middle of a field of predators to figure it out.

These predators must've had matching markings of their ass on a new chair for how long of periods of time they'd confessed of grinning all day. Sitting there from within his body daily, With TV monitors. Beings had names that rarely spoken left obvious suspicions of aggressive standards of movements towards the host. Yet very engaging in teachings that continued leaving small clues to life's real puzzles. Even an hall of formulas and fundamental science necessitates that would prove to be a foundation for further developments had been in a form gift by the same extraterrestrials who've in play tormented the worlds infancy.

Developments such as Eternal life. What seemed like a sale, brought interests in discovery and research that would then be secretly funded all over the world leading examples as study of Bone Marrow. It brought elements of vulgar hate to a innocent inhabitant. They grew jealous just at the thought of a young Hispanic mans now led on investigations and misguided bestowed apprenticeship from outer space.

Settled in reality that the world being greedy wanted in.

Wasn't just the interests of stories placed upon him. More of the science of appetite. Closed door interests of power hungry arms forces all over the map. Eclipsing new standards of understanding which did overlap genus of this era. Being too in mind, *if you want to better yourself check the company you keep*. Studying what they know and give, proving acquitted self defense necessary.

Levels, Halls, Rooms, Doors. What was behind that man remained a horror. Conglomerates of fakes and criminal masterminds. Urges of all came forth drinking a mans knowledge like water they'd drool over and steal. Like men, women of Sodom and Gomorrah. They'd bang those doors to force entry and see it. Thriving off of an others life out of fear. Miserable People.

Unintelligent over exaggerated strategists. It was a better conscious to insult them.

A real threat ever so present, yet at the wake of shift in pages of Earths history they presented themselves degenerating without further use of words. He was surrounded by vultures, criminal masterminds who for some reason had been given the powers to move advanced experimental weaponry shipped into space in irony aimed directly everyday pinpointed from morning to end. "There's just no way everyone is in part with this". Kid forced to shrug realization of how low some people really can be. High Authority as the enabler to utilize Satellites proved permission based and pressed on.

It was obviously led by occultists more then likely laughing at everyone in the background. Just over joyed watching someones life and legacy from their eyes while paying maximum to destroy this specimen of gifted interests. Useless had become of the Departments. There was no help when he called everyone in the country for answers and led forward investigations on the matter. Only to betray human reason along health and self love.

Of the invasive crowd now surrounding the young writer, guilt driven military had malformed itself. Tools to degradation, one specific weapon used is becoming as a cartoon in an artificial computing to mark the obvious of presence that they traced your thoughts. Cartoons directed at your brain to see out the corner of your eye, pretending to be devious and attack driven. Had it been used to make mad of a target. It was a hate crime driven assault and ended in attempted murder by failures.

There just wasn't any reason for secret weapons technologies to be present in Domestic territories. It would mean a pattern of infiltration had taken a foot at our door. Why these experimental weapons came to be allowed to reach the coasts had it been parked somewhere in our orbit. To be used for later. How dare of a group of grown men attack a younger man as racist fetish of sorts. Since the discovery and prolonged use of such, being caught in investigations of its use would more then obligate prison sentence to the abusers themselves. Spending time behind a cell was of non real interests as usual.

They all catered to it including some humanoids that came forth as alien in the presence of this telepathic like communications in an advance ship. Presenting unwelcoming attention of the details of controlled human identities. This sensual need of image and destruction was self disruptive. Goons, being pulled to be at naval command centers as informed, Submarines and Naval Destroyers packed these computers to work like a horse on a kid. Computers as a weapon had been a favored asset in the world of terrorism and mania. Like a pocket knife with multi use, had this little blade been the problem. Enemy of Mortal Men, had it been the impossible ghetto bird in space.

Being a vast of arsenals in military inventory, space technologies along computers to control them would bring only misery and murder in the streets. Experiments had been done, where someone would undergo a heart attack due to the electricity pulled and oxygen being built inside the chest. A shot of pain would also be introduced to 'tranquilize" at extent.

A certain design of these experimental eyes In the sky they'd launch was sold as terrestrial defense. Everyone bought onto it, including American military as precursor to the disasters. You could see the staggering amount of lawsuits that would come from this being aimed at the public consistently. Somehow it passed Senate and the Oval Office some time since the Space Race.

Dangerous and without real control, it didn't take long for the Department of Homeland security to get drunk and waste away at killing who they'd look at as issue to private agendas no one talked about in open. There being stories of migrants, darker skinned people and like as lighter being shot at with a satellite. It was shooting down on us, some people never getting up from bed dying of "mysterious illness/heart damage" The government took no case and considerations of their own safety.

Pushing out orders to murder "some more", being the only thing coming out in coherence of weakness. No real leadership was proven to be adequate in these circumstances. Yet there was money enriched devils of the world paying half a million for one of those satellites, traitors of the country would give in to it lavishly.

Everyone on the rock was looking for a savior and a father to look up to. It being laughable.

Space entities we're teaching the man "God of Destruction" killing off many space peoples they laughed at as vermin in the process. Yet punitive excessive sexual indulgence would follow onto everyone daily. It's how they thrived together and ate with eyes closed. Masturbating over our heads, to see a naked super model and thrive inside the husband or partner was a twitchy guy on a chair turned insect.

What an excuse for poor use of money. Talks rose of massive headaches and costs tens to hundreds of millions then further for the sensational mental breakdown of everyone running like bugs and coming right back to this perverted gala. When comfortable..

Lots of money to see a guy get twisted daily with computers and space monsters. All on private display, now being leaked, those that knew tuned in. Young Host knew he couldn't have been the only disturbed American Civilian from this phenomenon. Head Lines rang all over of a coming new Space dominance led by China. Having they lead the frontier of Hyper-sonic missiles and vehicles proved a challenge for the western world already.

Surrounded by unknown identities, connections government led with other corporate and parties needed something to catch up to their contenders. a classic crucifixion to see the devil summoned and a few guys on different colored horses and attire spread the end of the world. "It wanted to see it" Privately engaged with utilization of cold war and alien satellite technologies had been what they invested tremendously more on. Rather then actual measure of strength.

Being fiendish, Sensational appetite being celebrated. Kid said leave, didn't work nor budge he had already been forced to become of a sexual deal as others in a now CYBER-BRAIN- SLAVE-MARKET.. Wanting to see who he was having 'sexual intercourse" with, had become a filthy manner of pain inducement to him. They wanted his story to die and he rot with it. "THUS DID THE ACTION OF ULTI-MATE HUMAN BETRAYAL ARISE FROM A MIX OF POLITICS AND GOD". Rebellious others fought it.

Government sexual affairs, Documented secrets from the disastrous experimental procedures of such space technologies floating over the common public for decades. Manipulating the people since the dawn of the space age. Causing significant injury of both mental and physical health. It would mean collapse of the Republican Party and removal of their presence. Yet kept in the dark. Had treats been given out to lure the aliens for secret weaponry and information. Tall Talks and Tales of our ancients including of certain bloodlines that still roamed the Earth.

Warriors, scholars, to King Leonidas of the Spartan militia. Even science of planetary with grand studies of star life cycles control and hypothetical upkeep. Space traversal, interstellar lifestyles. It went on. Teams of professionals and dummies for practice aim is how new assembled private parties to watch this outer space threat. Some guys "mysteriously" got their cerebral cortex pulled down the brain by an inch or two losing conscious and some never waking back up.

Top ranked Psychologists from around the world had returned in secret to witness and give clarification as well instigate or be allowed questions to these foreigners from afar. This absorption became a elite challenge of survival and all a mash of art in a molecular level of god punch. It was taken, sipped and abused.

Near perfection, perfected mockery made at top efficiency to do the task at hand and gain details of anything possibly spoken about. It was in the air.

He got his "mentor" and he got a crowd of problems. This relationship was exotic and foul. like a cash grab, attached by needy. Several now Countries that had been involved, utilized computers as a weapon, Monsters had been biting their own tails, adorably. Then, Finally some light came forth. Enemies of the people had been downed, some removed of powers and prosecuted.

As far as how the rumors would go. Some Space Military training of the highest regards bestowed upon him an eye to view the mountains and terrains of what filth drove the Earth insane.

Damn good finds from all around the sectors of space. Protecting him. American leeches, Chinese mad scientists, Russian mob, Jewish money and alien. Bigger picture of who's doing it and whats going on. Policing the pyramid scheme, learning from it majorly. Yet was painful being given the need to move an initiative of ones own now stuck in forced institutionalization. "Them". It was the Illuminati itself, its members playing with aliens and satellites.

Highly encouraged to keep a distance, was ruled as rightful movements in these events. Illuminati had been told to keep away from the kid. Although the true reality was "What the hell we're they doing there". "I need everyone to leave"! It was said for years and again came with a heavy cost of a mans youth. Work being enacted too for following of these happenings and who was pointing what at who seemed to be played and mocked. How they had permission to bother was always the damn problem.

Investigations that did occur seemed to be motivated for reasons of running and hiding. Yet the young man asked, "Why weren't these results done before"? It was excuses after excuses. Separation of these hostilities from everywhere had to be done.

Everyone in the Department of Defense who knew of this was a hopeless coward and a fiend. For not telling families of potential threats.

As mentioned before it being necessary to take the absolute caution when determining intelligence of events that there fore would tremble the strong. With a hot list of masterminds in the cosmos now detailed. With names rarely ever given but amass of trove of information. Some Good money, other times dangerous. Each entity offered and invited to listen to extent enough to keep on eye on whats being categorized. That was just what present occurrences merged with a line of oddities on a kid could offer.

To Isolate, absorb and insult ethnics out of its simplicity. There was wild assortment of pawns, military's, militia, corporations, dictatorships, authoritarian like worshipers and its members. All both with a singular agenda to both bestow and keep a line of interests to indulge of others flesh in private. Even a Secret Government established as a branch around the world, being present pretending to have full control of this happening. Ill minded truths followed with need to decipher these new era intrusions.

Part of the deal they'd make, letting them to act on us.

~There was tales of men who dressed in reptilian bodies as their image of fear and warmongering. To keep away from that which lurked behind its walls and eccentric master craft of reign in a zone or sector. Claims even at a far off Galactic distance. A true Identity of these entities was the apparent origin being Hispanic like of indigenous species. A popular class of humanoid. Where thousand century year old technologically led people of all and warm climate ruled a vast of all space. It saw no color but well balanced in cosmic society.~

Royalty, families both recognized beautiful and regarded as mass heretics. Flawlessness abundant. "Architectos Del Arcaedies". Crafted knowledge users of the straw system of harvest.

They too cherished genetic splicing procedures. Kept many humanoid exotica as pets and sex labor. A class of big gulp and rule undying of thirst for more. With a armada of ships at plentiful planets through all they saw in the eye that roamed in heavens. It was that, they respected the boy. For those reasons to extent with praise. Taught him what they knew and cherished the bloodline of interests in a high ground view.

Roaming the Cosmos Many Men of Power Strong. Each observing and absorbing of their own Presence. Architecture having been massive in glimpse of what was detailed. Orbital ships in all Designer styles. Large following of an Eye and a pyramid, These Troves had detail of all mischievous labors to build and scale such heights. Building colonies on moons of planets with rocky rings.

They could see the mass of such environments of a gas giant from their neighborhood of greenery and stone, bio dome created homes, crafted from Eons of long hand work.

"Lo Eso"!

They'd call out. Humble

A society of strong men and women that recalled segregation as a standing point of excellence. Yet got lost in the sale of agonizing. How cruel these brothers and sisters must've been thrown into a mess of things. Especially in a mash of communications where true factors of intel, trade talks, articulate culture being always dismantled and disabled by a nature sense of space sabotage. POWERFUL is what everyone would call.

Massive bunkers housing computers in the instance being placed everywhere, the "ship sank soft" when they'd land. Mad science driven by hunger being the biggest downfall in space and reign.

Its this sexual appetite of things that murdered, eroding gluttony and disgust. Yet the mind of these pacts seemed broken and damaged from prolonged effects of technologies attached to them consistently, daily. As if there was no real care of what long term side effects these instruments have on one could be taken more accounted for with proper examinations. Yet the science ruled these societies, proclaimed themselves pinnacles of dexterity and patients. Grace was a walk only the rich could tap into. Proper maintaining of one another each had a welcomed conversation to the table and understanding being a key formula to everlasting rise of all. "Its a share of shit and gold". Said a voice of translation from this society.

Mad Gods of Science, Technology, Biological studies, Literature, Arts, Architecture, "Perverts" the most creepy. Its who controlled these communications and they stood among lurkers. "Elephants" coming out a joke, Artificial Intelligence Alias to dump Thinking and Health everywhere hand selected. Coming of the Neanderthal like of origin people these had been Generals of disruption. Laughing at all. Its image of an Elephant being more of odd newcomers habit to showoff mastered A.I. It was them that forwarded command of much. There was an idea that this was more of in fact a programmed teacher in a computer driven mechanical genius. "If I told you I get jokes from an Elephant would you believe me"?

CHAPTER XVI
"ITS THE ELEPHANT"!

"Un Elefante se Balanceaba," "Sobre la tela de una arana." "Como veia que resistia," "Fue a llamar a otro elefante!"

"Dos Elefantes se balanceaban," "Sobre La Tela De Una Arana." "Como veian Que Resistia," "Fueron A llamar a otro Elefante."
- Spanish Nursery Rhyme

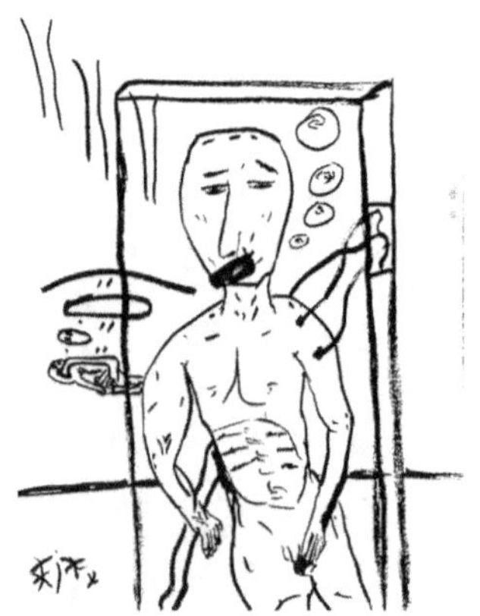

There are tales of Spartan Ancestry, Bathed in Wine. Where birthright to pass on ones bloodline is first without defect as an infant. Such a proud handsome group of people, Being obvious of what necessary elements kept the dominant lifestyles of Sparta lifted with legacy as time measured man. If those inspected noticed of anything other then "Healthy", what followed was death. Killing the infant was deemed the only step moving forward after it being carried for the estimate in a womb for nine months.

Membership exclusive order of the very most proud interesting figures of culture and planetary science groomed all kinds. Men especially being only of the best fit ,pushed of the envelope standard. It was Money. Gold. Liquid Water. Callings of wealth being only present in those sought as best in a masculine proclaimed owners of "Flesh and blood". Welcoming the young man to such divine worlds of "Knowledge and Power" with a branded original name as "Arcuitectos" They spoke of History and Future.

Mentors of "Space and Time". Bringing War home, desecration of what is "To Think". Christians of the modern world who leeched onto the young man both beloved and kept bay the persistence of how master salesmen clamored to the doors of Earth. These "Elephants" which was the preferred text they welcomed themselves masked. Carried balls to be so upfront about what they wanted here. Consistent skills of predatory nature, bluntly collecting all they pleased and craved.

Like the others in the circle of space horrors and science, wanted a taste of our women. They offered "Protection" to those that would follow with plans of world controlled schemes in which also perverted our peoples lives and sanity. They regardless gave their young host a sample of what they'd know with grand examples of the fruits in respect to work ethnic, Branded. Branded from century long space colonization's studies of good Eternal Life along the noted title of excellent, For the better.

We we're being invaded and Cthulhu was here, it was critical not to surrender anything. How unfortunate we got just that. An entire command, infantry, arsenal of "The United States of America and all its Departments" given to the hands of Extraterrestrials in secret. In Pop Culture and Conspiracy Theory there was consistent talks of these things. Like as themselves the "Illuminati", "New World Order". Cowards here real, more present in life then originally looked at in context.

Aliens rose and controlled our people, along everything else including, every step, monitored. White Nationalist being a most utilized pawns. It was laughable to see a Jew, A Nazi and a Redneck shooting laser bullets using satellites. Onto Blacks, Hispanics, everyone else they couldn't get along with. How distasteful, The Elephants along the centipede of other space oddities gave this third perspective narrative independently to the young host. A collaboration of others who at root Human, giving insight of our world to their belief..

They had the whole thing on lock. As far as all the Devils in a room used as mating supply later by other masters. How could aged civilizations from distant stars, catapult themselves low. Yet reaching peaks of ascension to par as hot as primordial Magma. It didn't sit right when you had a need of connectivity being an enabler to the brain sitting on a stem. A sign of implants with other science projects held the physical body with little thinking response coming from users. Terribly it was a major fault of evolutionary cravings to continue glorifying their own lives by the day.

It was these examples of how to come to the same standard of life as space dwellers such as "The Elephants" as they called themselves. To be as youthful and proud. Blunt and all knowing, those who are the Elephant of its image had been a league of extraordinary gentlemen and class of knowledgeable older species who've have already outgrown computers millenniums ago yet entrapped with them. A guild of scientists journeying as nomads.

Found in this network with other genetic experiments, other deformed creatures made to "push a button" and "pull the lever" while roaming an foreign atmosphere. Mashes of Deep Space Science came into scamming everyone of their freedoms and peace of mind. Monster Comedy for some arrogant prick. What started as a scheme led to creatures eating out of our brains in a mental disorder. Reminiscent to cannibalism. They engulfed memories and feelings of us in secret while marketing to ancient space mobsters. All gang affiliated, Having their own codes and trust networks similar to what was found here on Earth.

Ethnics in presence was laughable knowing how hypocritically and undesirably rules of sustainable guidance being unbound to those that pushed such standards of living. Witnesses on Earth had believed there could be a downfall of a slope in some of these civilizations that gathered and hacked their way in these networks like that existing on our planet. Living Healthy, Humble, Graceful, Intelligent and orderly. Proper foundations for life and family. Business and sportsmanship. These sort of traits and behaviors seemed almost non existent with other civilizations come across, in the network of channels these monsters in the attic carried. Made to harvest and push the money was littered everywhere as man scouted these channels.

In that network came fixed filters from other planetary outposts where rigorous attacks of strategy having debilitating effects. Trojan horses sold it to the cold war men in arms, from otherwise enticement following secret introductions of variant mysterious of origin, groups. Bartering, Giving news of recent events through ship signal links, Data blueprints of goods and merchandise, Passing Elephant jokes as well intel, there was abundance in this. Paradise wasn't set without flaws to a service in the space of Eden. There was little care of how these signals and links might have triggered effects on other planets environments, as they'd pass through the mantle of a world. Magnetic Sphere for instance could not be under looked.

Present need of hijacking insured rushed progression on unique endeavors that would otherwise promote more unsafe sustainability. An old favorite, spamming bribing tools. Such example of sending pornography to an otherwise expendable of a network labor monitor always thirsty and needy of nude beautiful women. Once this Monitor in charge would see gifts of pornography on a screen it had them hot with need for more.

Allowing further access and data sharing. Such was the Elephants. A program and a mentor of its own working while teaching the young host, a snip of how everyone played.

"If I told you an Red Elephant tells me jokes everyday would you believe me?" Says the young man to his coworkers. Already at this point opened quite wide of his endeavors with the paranormal in which otherwise forced in. "There was an Elephant pumping air into a balloon and the balloon kept taking him up and up higher then before", "I swear I never saw it pop". After all, this imaginary mentor of his reminded him of noting whatever was seen down.

These sort of gifts and curses are rare in life. No where in human history was there presence of kids talking to strange things that shared their needs and knowledge with while it lasted. Being very defensive on the experience was highly needed in these steps. Precautions given and what to do with, semi controlled by other interests more Earthly in which of whom only sought to keep these certain keys and space talk elements at all times closed door. Never to speak of imaginary friends to the legislative communities whom too being meddled in surveillance by Red Elephant Republican military grassroots.

Artificial display following meditation directed at God, having crafted unique programs to both polish and teach the young man of being more importantly a Legitimate master of his own. After all that was a gift of excellent prayer. Such teacher would be better vocally contracted. It was these mentors and military procedure like movements lead world conquests by the sector of dark space.

How anyone could eat in such environments or sleep in a bed at home was colder and uneasy. When there was understanding of the largest land animals floating around our heads everyday staring hard at families for fetish. Far from Hindu God of Wisdom, Ganesha. Salesmen claimed ancestry to some manner to the start of such symbolism found abundant in our cultured societies. "In the past everyone was more sophisticated and intelligent". Being said of this, another side of investigations would lead again to the belief that after some time, everything was too deprived.

Hippocampus of a host left damaged due to the penetrative nature of signals from outer space technologies. Either they didn't care to explain the detailed side effects deriving from such. Being present in all space of which utilized these instruments from the get go proved to be dim witted. It did in fact rot the brains neuron transmitters. Waves being heavy enough to slowly have information disengage itself from other reflexes found to be more natural. Yanking his notes there was nothing that could be done.

Speaking of which as the Elephant said. "Dark matter is a isotope". A combination of aged elements, minerals everywhere. Time had did this to us. Rarely ever answering questions, everything said was to be written as quick as catching a train.

Autonomous teaching tool and biological rounded insignia. It was this image that was selected to distribute troves of answers pacing the network at advantage where everything grappled control of the ships and satellites links.

Of "extraterrestrial presence" arrived and parked here on the solar system. Space loves Menageries, An organization devoted to collecting clues of endangered and unique species on each planet like an expensive hobby. Nothing on Earth came near or par to the intricacy these species of different origin delivered in detail. Having a flying Saucer been a alien exotic satellite of its own. If only it weren't so damn parasitic of a system. Keeping record still to remain on guard of our mythical miracles in the attic.

Conversation would go dark without straying far from how things from space lived in our bodies in secret. High need to control our nervous systems. It was the point of this market. Even the elephant being a biological mess and advanced computer system had his share of the hosts women when he'd bed her. If not him, someones love life being ravaged and mutilated the same.

These beings of Authentic flare loved war and control. Knowing how to round them up added a long study and note of its own, even by the elite hired to register, working as they wore a white coat of that which presented itself in expensive research.

Having hints these arena ready champions dominated the network at our bay. Claims of advance teachings to otherwise "hand selected" newcomers. Species, with evidence again originating from homo-sapient like our own. Glorified trophies in their treasure rooms of what these "Arquitectos" eroded. Having all had a unique trait and showcase of what progress led team efficiency to traverse the stars at a long shot. Such as themselves "biologically advance deep space scuba divers".

One in particular of interests a being with a trunk attached to the mouth, connected to the belly. A creation of these "Elephants", Stationary in a ship traveling at warp speed, survival dependent of its stomach full and plump. Moment the being was launched, It would not come back. Like as regurgitation, A cycle of mush and saliva itself hydrated, fed full. Damn thing still looked malnourished, Yet claiming to be a pinnacle of hand work.

There wasn't an answer how far its been diving for everything about it still ticked. A Richard Mille, Their "Space Scuba Diver" is a hand-crafted Gem. It was the purpose to survive far away as possible. For as long as possible. As Fast as Possible. That had been the goal had it was pushing over ten years in space traversal accelerating 2.5x the speed of light. Its TOP.

Bouncing over the web of space networks otherworldly claimed control over. Masses of these Elephants as they called themselves encouraged advance study of everything. Deep pockets and eccentric personality, aided them to standout in the crowd of different bodies. Respected and marked as a private party of legendary intelligence. A collection of Music, Imagery, Facts, History, Fruits of worlds as the telescope could see.

Being sought after needs to fill their own data banks. So many being inline to follow the same example as the large footprints left by its creative community from afar. Key fisher(data hoarders) groups in the same party who used the lure tactic, Left a strain of different alien network computer doors once fortified now forced open. It's because of how these knobs had been left twisted, audaciously calling to otherwise unwanted attention of something else. Since a post breach of beings as followers to them continued the hustle. Amassing more nomadic intrusion to repeat an entry as sold by likes of Key Fishers themselves.

To think it was these things that too controlled mass world maneuverability and mayhem. They'd sell themselves as innocent but bullied all to shit. Even uproars in the East such as the Russian Invasion of Ukraine being centered as a show watched by the Aliens and outrun personal, hired to do their bidding by Government and Military Manipulated Elite.. Controlling infantry decision making, enacted on civilians.

Space had to Die. Sworn that these beings lurked behind it.

Meanwhile N.A.T.O, other more private groups in American government and military. Embracing these new odd humanoids to utilize their powers for warmongering when contact had established. Unfortunately in disgrace letting out these attacks using satellites had been given to extraterrestrials. Even full advantage of their capabilities, technologies synchronizing to Ukraine civilians, everyone under left targeted. Implementing their own needs and frenzy in a war zone of all things.

Terribly this, the host was told and given of detail showing how dominating tactics had been given to extraterrestrials, willingly as his eyes closed shut throughout his home in this form of cybernetic meditation. Seemed to be almost too ordinary or of common practice, for leisured "gift giving". Watching the media gave no laughter. There then similar articles of an unusual increase of rape onto women and children of Ukraine by Russian front line infantry as an invasion already at a start coming from the East. Media spoke about it for weeks.

These details popped up by the tens to hundreds. So many beautiful innocent people murdered with attacks from the sky, while crying to Christ. Responsibility was blinded by the money, why these humanoids we're allowed this was the bigger problem. Who in a large party or agency behind the curtain would target innocent in such a grotesque manner and claim it strategy.

Russian military's being blamed, the easier approach, still a closed door deal. True Mr. Lector was space, that was of whom was pulling the "Shit on the walls" in Ukraine's Borders as well as putting the rest of the world at risk of another World War. Had it all been manipulated onto Russian plotting since the beginning, enacted capabilities of idea tampering and artificial aggression build up.

Ironically "The Elephants" being of its elusive nature, Qualified as a real mark of genius that presented this evidence along side handfuls of others from the cosmos. To allow true information to pass on to wordiness. In a hint leaving a since of good and spontaneous sarcasm. Yet never believe anyone foolish. Had it not been a scout with advance space capabilities that which triggered other schemes. A finesse towards ever numb Agencies affiliated in foreign affairs. If the Elephant itself was an actual being rather then Artificial Intelligence was always a shroud of mystery.

Claiming indigenous ancestry where moral discipline of physical restrictions towards another, been absent.

INTELLECTUAL DOMINANCE ARISING FROM ABUSE

Given perspective and asked opinion of what the young man thought of the intruders. Damage onto man itself from precursors of the stars that once resembled our own. If they truly look like us. "This is evil, now to give this information out and follow with observation". An intelligence and informative had been entrusted out of the student.

Brunette of hair and facial complexions, be not as unique as we previously theorized. Again, we found the source of what was shooting at our star to such force projecting solar flares and direct strikes on our planets ozone. In effects of the early 2020s, news struck of new communications such as the Star-link satellites respectfully, also receiving loss of system functions.

Capabilities too. Strategy of them to have higher ground as the "Art of War" claimed overlapping powers. Presence overseeing what is below. Being ours and others worldlier tools and instruments. Noting mental damage have had a toll in the youth of a spacemen. Had they involved Military branches in a twisted deal now overrun by bio weaponized racist in the modern world left communities in mysterious absence of comfortable peace.

<u>All of space is sabotaged.</u>

Smacking the light from hate was a stricken match enough. Leaving our Suns natural elements degrading with high anxiety, the worlds bugs now forced to follow the job previously handed to them. Audacity for the domestic strength of our nation to be handled by poor minded nationalist and hate enthused psychopaths. Blind and Blunt, it was pressured onto them to approach this more openly onto the public in an orderly fashion if they had it in them. In signs of sigh, they couldn't, wouldn't thought shouldn't have to. They felt a tactical advantage of sorts if they left these matters foolishly small to a handful with responsibilities.

Enforcing a "Doom Bringer" to take full advantage of money and torture of the young man who alerted all intelligence in the Country. Blindly shooting the kid instead.

Fear rose. "At the end of the day you looked at the ground and thought I Shoulda, I Coulda, I Woulda." Being the response he'd reply to his misogynists the Department of Defense so proudly left him with. Screams rose of torture on his head with massive computers attempting to murder. A half of what strategy these disgusting people could conceive. As if that's all they could think about without any shame. Many entities did not know what to do of it. How to better protect the guy in danger, having the host being targeted by everyone whom betrayed humility.

People of innocence under the eyes of a God mutilated of the life they could've had. Found to be the true affiliate to be those responsible for protecting and promoting peace. "To exchange for Alien secrets, blueprints and information of an eternal elixir". In the mix had it hyped aggression for spending too much time with them. Produce of vomit for these actions to be surrounding present society. They feared the boy because of the truth he carried, absurd. Elephant quickly tells the young man and his predatory stalkers in command centers "Study bone marrow, fertilizer". As if basics to extend life's longevity in flesh and blood. Our world in havoc and comedic that teachings had still been given.

Flesh of my Flesh, Blood of my Blood. It was an Elephant with jokes that brought order and intelligence in a place of precious dogma had it been the idea. Yet in space with body(s) being a major high market, It left everyone who knew of these disasters to embrace the game of sex sells. Story behind the massive military control of women, men and a nation wide human smuggling ring using agencies like the Federal Bureau of Investigations as a cover up tool. While people went missing and dead naked women found on the carpet. Computers had still lurked everywhere, including the Great Wall of China Housed these servers. Our Star and Planet being shot at from a distant aggregator and groups gaining leverage.

"What else could possibly be going wrong" followed with a nervous Thank you.

Young Girls abducted from all over the world strapped onto beds in Guantanamo Bay secret facilities. Taken from their families crossing the border for just happening to be pretty. Large dildos and sex machines controlled by agents, scientists, rich elderly and aliens would push a button as children lost their virginity's to a team of supremacist and criminals. They wouldn't eat, leaving them bone dry of muscle or proper nourishment. Young host being a forced witness in his sleep waking up in sweats of these visions and stories.

Kids from Puerto Rico shot right on the spot, when the discovery was called, by the young man for Guantanamo bays standing bases to investigate. Naval would show up first and take little girls out dumping their corpses somewhere even forced underground. Mothers left crying scared and unhinged on where their daughters went now missing. Leaving a plate full and empty of their presence. American Military commanders flourished in this shit and stood up exhausted when their names would be called out for inspection.

Strong presence in otherworldly had dominated without a fact these people. In turn left succumbed into treason with cold war codes and pamphlets. Left as the rules to diminish true work of initiative and carry of code nation ethnics. To think some of the colonels would come home to a medal being in league with these unruly subjects for decades. Its one thing you know about it and reject the obvious, announce it before it happens. Poor case of failed reason in effect the complete mishaps of standard, thus a manipulated embrace of such stupendous actions.

Threats had increased, bewildered. "It's what military's have been doing for hundreds of years even eons". Said a poor minded fool with a rifle and a name. Never given, as if what he was saying out to the young man had any worth coming from his mouth.

Suckers in the Government had justified Rape onto man, "! Because it's what military's have been doing for hundreds of years!" How, could they follow. While on the outlines, It was this so called mentor of a branch that had in revelation all the algorithms himself to kill on command. Why implement dishonor onto himself and others so

Klutz by not doing the initiative to remove such bio weapons targeting innocent.

Limited Powers had stricken the odds of peace, there was little anyone could do. Yet an abundance of evils was always around. It was the guy with the big red button himself controlling everything under it. We are taught so mastered, unexpected from others, all around, and a talking Elephant to be the presence who shares this.

CHAPTER XVII
"PIG-MENTATION"

- A Natural COLOR of skin in animals, or plants.

It wasn't unusual to listen to the chatter in public schools as huffs and smacking riddled some of the other classmates.

Especially in certain rooms gifting American History. A need rather than a want, as a means to maintain remembrance of our ancestors labor. Being rare of an interest for younger children as well as adults. Yet it was these courses in fact stood out as a mark of golden eras to what made where we are, more what we have as privilege.

A few studies leading, informed of movements preexisting all over the country. Which of some encouraged to speak up against that which counters Freedom. It's what this country is all about.

Represented for centuries, this champagne of air in our lives is the sun kissing it. When it came to the shades of colored, Negros as the Spanish called them. Darker toned men and women of our human legacy. Brought brilliance of how the stretch of life on Earth goes to such extent to create varieties. On the desk some heads we're laid down hearing it. It was boredom and spoilage of the free glass handed as a given. Slavery, Rosa Parks, Lincoln even our forefathers as time went back. All had a connection to the call of liberty and its sweat.

At the mist of a time when another confused familiar brethren of sorts. Pushed the mile to blast you, it was the watch of discipline to resonate a force of action. Cause and Effect, watching slideshows while we wrote notes of these events had to be concreted to us. "Write Notes" mirroring as the book had. Some of it still shrouded by ambiguous facts. Regardless it helped us, maintained our center and respect as "what we already knew" to be the obvious after teaching. It's how it feels when you study and know it better than anyone else. A lot of good people hit in the head those apparent days, some for the faults of skin pigmentation. Such a peculiar thing for modern day society. Kid didn't know these sort of behaviors being so actively present from older generations carrying it. A lesson to a migrant with a blind eye in extent. Innocence unnoticeable of foolish segregation.

As a child the hustle was real. You had to be excellent in some traits to stand out from beyond any obstacles of the "octagon". Lands foundations of concrete and steel. You had to fight if anything. Some got twisted up with mobs and gangs rather then a stand of other options that if you search you will find.

Bloods, Crips, Republicans and Democrats. Affiliations of either had all been the same. You we're checked and identified of details along colors of the trace to represent you for the rest of your life.

Having to pick one was a problem. Which team do you go for? Which side are you on! Learn something from it. Live from it. If your true identity is strong it will resist some temptations of turning against your humble structure. Being the most important, what makes your life more attentive to public identity.

Living a life as an introvert or open market big gamer. Having an eye for details on the welcome benefits of quality air. Peacefully consistent to what giving and receiving, Being a shadow a chameleon. Changing its colors dependent of its environment.

Welcoming the reflex as a skill of who you are is a master of its own. Living peacefully with this conjoined twin to make one, you ate the weak of you making yourself stand larger among those with anxiety to be around people. It's how a lot of successful global market leaders became so interesting. They don't even show off the goods they acquire just consistency being prevalent. It's the relation with the surroundings that aids the kid to live. This point was unordinary.

"Beaner"!, Called a slithering space reptile to the kid. "I don't even eat beans that often, fuck off". "lemme get some of that", the entity would beckon as it mimics the boys lips smacking and chewing. What a nerve. As the young host looks at his dish after it being microwaved. Damn thing was on him and the rest of whatever followed him like a line of oddities. He finishes quickly even exampling actions as if he takes a shot of shooting a loogy on his food. What horror for someone to have such efforts simply to enjoy his own meal.

It's been several years daily of these space hazards on his plate. Consequently of daily changes to his behavior depending of the abusive and unreal teachings aliens offered. It was a damn sale but some of those notes he had written over the time proved realistically, to be of very keen interests with legitimate details.

Reading through those papers in essence some of the shit had real facts. Understandably plenty of it only came as defensive writing to the foes that presented themselves from the day he started moving that pen, marker and pencil.

"Colonel's!, Leave that boy alone"! Voices crying out in his head of investigations following up the trail in secret. It seemed, Government officials finally got a hold of some of these tyrants in the same military's personal stationed with access of dangerous capabilities. Including the radio systems and links to space technologies, that would be sent out via hidden projection instruments found on the ground maintained by an operator. "He was trying to kill white people!" the liar would call. It was this operator one of many whom targeted civilians. It was of upmost urgency to remove such terrorists.

"They gave us so much stuff"!, UN-flattered to hear the boy listen to the operator screech from the side of his own microphone to only attack his mind. Young man remaining quiet listening to what was being passed along in these alien espionage network.

Having been the trade of human slaves for personal destruction. Weapons and notes more hints to secret buried gold and treasures.

It's another reason the branches sold themselves to the things under the bed. It would last long regardless, E.T counter parts seemed to be giving the boy third perspective by force in some torturing ritual of mentorship. As If testing his survival and twisting a person they have no relation with. This terrible situation had to come to some close, not without a massive amount of shared intelligence. After all wouldn't that have been a shame not to get anything from this.

Moving slow, it was hard enough to know some of the men in the Departments in America being in bed with these things.

Claiming preference to eliminate the young man rather than to have let him go in the first place. Undeniable showcase that this was how some of them ate together. Stretch the flesh and mind of innocent, how vile. Even when some a few officers including links to Generals in the Pentagon claimed they preferred working with Neo Nazis. Befalling into a trap to lure generations of top ranks to welcome otherwise members of the public with a history to divide the people.

Thus offering such military equipment and funds from the yearly budget to close door offerings. Such heart break for the roots of evil to come from those that promised to protect. It was they out of a B-Rated movie that in fact did exist, disabling our interests of real liberty. Being a different world in actuality in comparison to what we find in open public. What was considered a more elite group of people were none other then Ex Military and Espionage figures entangled by this sinister persona from space too. Had given enough evidence to support the claims as a whole of actions to be held accountable. People just fueling fire to a flame that would prove more then catastrophic to our future and present day doings. Groups of segregated power, possessed beings, consumed in the head to entrap while rising hate to another human being. Without having any real connection with them.

It wasn't unusual to hear about this now that the reality of things was coming to motion. More of these "Colonels" as men with an alias would pop up daily. Threatening to shoot the young host for fears of information posing a threat to military branches preservation(s). Eating of the public with Aliens had more power then the President as whole. They, having more of these monsters roaming and staging the whole thing. Simply for some of the present day members of our Countries Defenses along the hands they shook, make their own get away. To avoid Prosecutions.

At one point kid had to rush and pull things out the fridge.

They had provoked problems again, so best to defend himself behind the refrigerator doors, hoping to shield himself inside it. In Hopes the ice and material would shield his body as a microwave attack was being focused around his neck like a noose proving they'd slice it off if they "really wanted to". In manner of fazing from outer space in a combination of maltreatment and display of their UN-favored act of cruelty onto him. It's a damn good thing he put the effort in, enough to shock the eyes of those witnessing it.

They all wanted to escape, while pointing blame at victims was a "obvious plot". **Having everyone hostage at this point by satellites controlled by Alien Masters and extremists** in secret, been such uneasy of a life. This was being contained, it was out of control and the strategy behind it being such a damn twisted horror. Kid calls out for anyone there to kill everything harming another. He knew he had not been alone and some of the guards these entities or people had did in fact risk themselves to save lives.

They'd all go insane and it was for dire importance to remove these degenerates at haste. After all, being surrounded by mentally unstable with such advanced experimental capabilities was a complete no-no. It had to die. Everyone's life was at this point at risk. Some of the talks roamed how control had been held back. Many of the operators, found drunk and drugged utilizing such things having an upper hand claimed Gods illegitimacy.

On the other hand, our star had been critically shot at by foreign weapons technologies. Mysterious solar flare events had now multiplied and the investigators had too much of a hand full. China had become a culprit to place blame of degeneration. Fault of failed foreign affairs Pentagon begs, asking China and other nations around the world to aid in removing the victims while they ran off warm and comfortable for the next batch of insults they had carried on a case to produce.

Fortunately, they couldn't even touch the poor guy. Just enough to embarrass one another. Perverted people even had the computer servers set to punish the innocence autonomously. A full plastic object of shape in which multiple computers linked in space instruments attached to someones location to stalk, insult, piss over in laughter pressed rigorously.

Maniacal mischievous menace, Complete ugly. No one had any self control and it was for the better of all things for these parasites to finally be laid to rest. In fact, wasn't just white supremacist in a bubble, they had done it to the Asian, Chinese other eastern counterparts to maintain dominance of terror attacks a reason to misguide all those in efforts to close a case. In part, lack of understanding colors had been the fuel of these issues.

Those that spoke Mandarin we're playing everyone and the racists in the west falling. Still watching from afar, claims one or the other cried to the skies for "help", but the damn things so punitive of the mind, Put themselves in these situations. *"It's his fault, I hate him so much"!* Had the show gone sour, hearing cries from the fires of hell. Running from the inevitable, Pigs. To think they used such things as semi-conductors and satellites to intoxicate women and masturbate every damn day drooling over what they couldn't bed with.

Legislation in America had already suffered the most of it.

Being burden with bad reports and head injury from similar satellite terrorism. Being unknowing of things at such last minute. Media and news proved of how inadequate these people paved the image for themselves. Abortion was what was used as a hot topic to control public information and keep another failed presidential administration alive to an audience. Only running behind the question of killing an "embryo or not?" An entire party of members somehow dormant in status to deliver as usual yet using Abortion as a means to seem active.

Yet kept it to themselves and ran the other way while tyrant man temporarily controlled the world as planned with space men. Dreadfully enough the scene of them hoping abortion proceedings would be enough to show their presence for the people. Entire lives at stake and they all held to the belief, already a handful, Department scarecrows would be enough to fight time itself. We we're surrounded and none of the older generations came to the line of reality of it.

Our towns we're under attack. Our Government, being responsible yet undesirably lazy to fix what damage they and the military did. With unlimited funds they gave it up to a small batch of crews by the day. Not foreseeing how critical it was to keep out these intruders wanting to control, destroy, corrupt our land and country. Over this dilemma, "Kill the kid"!! these pests taunted daily. As if killing him would prove to change anything. Again it was reminded of him to be at his best behavior and be a good listener, or else face damnation of the wicked ever so watching him.

At this point the boy had guns pointed at him from space and near home. Area of his surrounding's had been so bugged with members of different groups around the world maintaining eyes on the guy. Going to work back and forth was a challenge itself with interference of everything bashing at him using psychotronic weaponry. Horror movies filled the atmosphere of alien spam and hate rooted men on the ground. Locked tight on his head for several days, months turned years.

United States Government and military placed in agreement the decision to market public society as interests for trades with Extraterrestrials. A number exact was to be of hundreds of thousands to millions over the span of fifty plus consecutive years. Offers of people's lives and memories captured with advanced experimental technologies. In which roam in our aerospace and space sectors in a combination that would trigger secret wars with procreated "controlled" investigations over the years.

Had it been the only thing that kept everyone so silent on the matters. Fears of consequence to those producing it. Had it caused laughter and frustration. When the time had come for cuffs and bullets, no one dared move on it. For much of the extremist movement itself been overpowered and bloated now with the addition to the "Space Force" twisted games of mind control.

Mentioning the branch had been one of the primary traitor hubs collecting human data secretly with split controls while a satellite hovered over us, a dealing with Homeland Security as swell going the extra mile with other departments. Unfortunately, there was no time wasted for these intruders to establish themselves with a new rank and chair. Furniture was the only thing that changed for any true allied powers, while enemies toggled minds who've brought light into the room.

A sacred life was no more, addicts and drunkenness of deep space creatures had entered our homes in the dark. Russian Infantry had found its way inside our heads and homes using the same satellites out of a private illegal dealing. Such a waste, the occult's on Earth spent the waking hours of the day parading torture for these specimens.

Kid was being attacked and no one in the government would give him a hand nor return a phone call. What you would call cowards. Situation was getting worse, the investigations proved to be too slow. Lives on the balance of murderers who claimed powers even hand of **Presidential Cabinet** members. Results of ill minded terrorists and uncultured devoting their lives to satanism and aliens. Even the Grand Wizards of the modern era went into hiding. Celebrating glory of People chasing colors their entire lives. Watching us from behind our cellphone.

Such of (N.S.A) National Surveillance Agency itself including likes of Homeland security and those they spread word of how to utilize powers for personal pleasure. Uncalled for activity of the

highest degree, with need to consistently break the activities down along others to see. Going as far now as looking at life through out bodies perception of view.

Root of it being alien. Man turned horrors of evolution for a high inside a box. Most of these space vermin twisted by centuries of sabotage along criminal syndicates. Yearning for another day they went into computers and robotics in hopes to live a little longer and indulge as such. Placing insist that they could live forever this way in a hibernation chamber.

Its what started the adrenaline of these supremacists hidden within military being used as bio weapons against us for the aliens, controlling thoughts and ideas. Since the first incidents to evoke interests such as the "Roswell accident". Led to it being in fact strategic, as means to enter the military, with entertained forced interests of redesigning more then just blueprints put in product.

It was said a German known as Adolf Hitler instigated to some degree the second World War, A German known as Oppenheimer ended it. Foreign entities had indeed been the culprit

,previous gen programs during our mid nineteenth century. Being studied that Germans had been in an alien space program synchronized because of a favored pleasure of choice for aliens. Craft from outer space secretly researched and confiscated. Just like that found on Roswell, of different unique structures and hieroglyphic like patterns pressed on their material. There was just no reason to believe it was of another foreign adversary like we've been accustomed to find here on Earth.

Everyone seemed to have grasp of these materials, craft or objects settling somewhere near buried under the dirt for some time. Dig Sites with secret Nazi wars, predestining though the decades. Catching the interests of Private organizations with small armies and high end assassins. Something clouded the air of these separate lifestyles who had all been slowly transformed by

the hypnosis present of mystery.

Gorilla tactics squeezed the bugs dry of fluid and knowledge, those that had grown time with the enemy, soon became like them and familiar. It was through science and further conducted experiments of wreckage and trove collecting, that these objects now came in the form of Signal transmitting and capturing satellites causing a space race that would other wise go out of hand.

Urges got the best of everyone, in particular people of classified colored, had been the best example of experimented public attacks. Once they saw the effects of what these experiments in secret did to the people, had it grounded the communities as a whole to the ground. It was a complete set up from outer-space and Soviet to American secret space deformity attacks. They wanted the world to engineer these things, Soon overpowering our then amateur sophisticated approach to space endeavors. Confusing strategy and science for further development with the people now burden onto the future..

"You should probably recruit more", "Think of it this way, if your village is undergoing an attack, you alert your fellow men!" "With need to recruit"! Says the young man to his cybernetic jailers of the military. "It is of upmost urgency we get to it. We are facing problems that don't make since to the common man because hes uninformed of the reality we all face". "I even suggest getting warehouse workers to build sufficient ships in the mean time to patrol and remove hostilities from our atmosphere and surrounding environment, getting the whole Nation involved!".

Even at an amateur level of bribing and cunningly getting someone to agree with his side. His attempts had proven futile for the computers held his brain and body with others for them to listen by force. How could it freedom be if his room was filled with Nazis and Aliens. Yet some secrets did portray the reason behind this predicament. For even a racist military operative opened up that we had been already invaded and much of these procedures was out of everyone's hands. As many felt they had no choice but to break him out of fear.

It had come to attention that the entire time since the discovery of wreckage and knowledge of other existence. Having immediately been brainwashed as soon as teams or groups had been ordered to check the premises of a sight in discovery. Having confused in totality those on board the motive to filter these findings. Having been very limited actions to better safe guard our Nation. How foolish it was for these branches to have done so little to improve our safety and find otherwise fundamental routes that would prove better. As in a never devised plan to built an armada of ships with American or Migrant Men on call for our own protections. It was too late everyone head was in a box or lost in a trance of sorts. Not to mention being entangled further would permanently morph personal thinking into something else.

Numbers soon becoming against our side, being clear there was more overwhelming powers in root of it. Codes of conduct and rules make shifted in Departments, forced few people to only know of these issues. A consistent need to withhold proper global understanding of what we're surrounded with. "Modern day racist", wanted in and only they had permission to access this information. Wanting to play God by alienating our own nation of people from one another, seeing these space technologies for themselves in action was enough to utilize themselves. Thus then pushing human future procedures in spiral, sabotaging everything and everyone bluntly pointed the finger at the other.

Early ages of space conquest was set back by the dilemma of the cold war. Classified marked accidents created tensions that other wise had clustered the files they locked up. Inevitably the fire was rising, No one wanted to take responsibility and yet organized groups wanted watch of whatever else was out here kept small.

America left vulnerable, so was the world. Take it as, Our City was being attacked by monsters in secret and no one was telling the people. Everyone was being programmed tight mouthed and muted. Strategy was failing, leadership doomed us.

Hard hitting introductions of Mob affiliations interfering with government and foreign relations. Waters of the sinners in which the demons drank, bathed in privacy. White brainwash, now a modern joke of bleaching the world. "Could've left the cloth orange", "Couldn't have any of that", Some of the space dwellers and societies would think. Being accustomed to seeing no evil in a time of innocence long in the past before any prospering community endorsed a microchip.

Blended back the color that much of, took out. It was necessary to see proper procedure to act on what interference roamed the air. Places in America suffered extreme toxicity of brain damaging side effects, intensifying outcries of non-reasoned anger and frustration in communities. People felt sick of something and couldn't put a thought into what the problem was. Things left in silence which would other wise brought out. Left better safety measures and laws that could garner prosperous rule of ethnic stability.

America was being under attack and it was more domestic then over sought outside. Ringing in the ears could be heard in some people, coming as tinnitus, reality was these signals and frequencies bouncing all over the place.

CHAPTER XVIII
"SECRET KNOWLEDGE"

Books, Books, Books so many, Books so Few.

"The more you know, the less there are"
- JLR-J

Birds and the Bees, there was startling evidence being noticed of satellite and radio waves potentially effecting the ecosystem as well as vegetation globally. Feathered geese absent to some areas flying south for the winter, local birds starting to chirp fewer occasions in the morning including throughout the day. Bees seen less then the abundance collecting pollen in the spring and summer, making way to the hive being seemingly problematic.

Even the beautiful Monarch butterfly in Michoacan, Mexico showing evidence of fewer numbers turning up to the migration in its natural bio dome. Being blamed at as climate change, it was these signals pouncing the cause of instability. Government restorations couldn't seem to bring about the ability for these insects to a natural level of normal numbers. Dropping some fifteen percent in the past decade or so, regardless steep of a decline better seeing to.

Measures to the day had to be given as to means of stabilization. Everyone was stuck wanting to figure an answer out of these marks of interest in climate shifts. Temperature rising because of space beam attacks and other sophisticated signals pointed at Earth was becoming a sight of reality. Warming up wasn't the cause of oil and rise of emissions to some extent. Better case of when the Earth being filled with magma and volcanic sulfur before animistic prehistoric eras took route.

Our world regardless breathable, flourishing of life itself to take up. Carbon dioxide was abundant and trees love it. It's what they eat and grow out of. "Climate Change is a Hoax", truth is the planet was under attack from foreign weaponry. Intelligence in this age knew little of it, the kid was being told all of it in his bedroom. Months of shared research and intelligence for him to get a use of and double checked reassurance to share with others. These numbers applied to poor science. Being demonstrated with little regard of a potential hazard. In which otherwise would garner more issues if found uncontrollable, like as similar to a nuclear disaster.

It would've been unwise not to offer more insight and rational perceived ideas of better handling with anyone. "Where do I start"? "Government noses we're on his day getting in the way and defaming him". Clumsy and slow, their lives themselves had something other of an antagonist behind other motives as a challenge. Proper communications had been absent, secret absorption of his life. Intelligence being mashed caused a poorer excuse of time and exercise during cataclysm. You could take notice of a reason mostly being the rise of understanding that our neighborhood in the stars was more alive then we previously imagined. Unfortunately contaminated from post disgrace and sabotage driven perversions of their ancestors.

Perversions of mania had drunkenness disturbing the people and its peace. A student in rare teaching had been distastefully labeled a criminal by the United States Justice Department for standing his ground, yet still protected by rights. Quest for Secret Knowledge had found biblical folklore characters pouncing in his room for more. Christians of hypocritical frame had no image other then a cartoon named trouble. Puzzling sight to see an occasional drift of information being poured onto a random inhabitant.

Necessary in part for an addition to the case of human understanding, that there was a way to see other people from inside another body. Connected to their brain plugged vice-versa and space got lost in it. People as a totality had been victimized.

Had it been those swearing up and down of protecting society being in league with re-engineered alien weapons pointed at out heads. It was these Satellites now autonomously defending itself while its arms grabbed our minds and whereabouts with everyone's favorite pocket tool being a cellular device. They didn't just track us with one, they potentially could live in our brains with such *signals near our bodies* sending and receiving data consistently. Secret Knowledge was the Private thinking of the people. We in a modern society with established laws would know to do better.

That caused a hidden panic that was felt all over the Country's scrutinized men at arms. Hidden criminals using every excuse to *arrest him*, Wasting time and another mans comfort where ever he went. They had nothing on the guy, it was a clear indication of distorted powers. A Illuminati plot had gone haywire and soiled. No one having account of thee responsibilities given, poorly have been distributed, disregarded. Dumbfounded, some we're around to simply leisure out of human misery and it was chased plenty of occasions, evidence stored under a United States BLACK VAULT. Good to have knowledge of, what bumped in the dark wasn't of Gods Plans.

Military's being paid hundreds of thousands to millions under the table to keep a torture show ongoing of young people being dishonored. Justice was slow yet the day consisted of brain eating out of one person. Sexual Predators had been winning the game of law and order. Some racist others trigger happy naive.

Dangerous.

"I'd like to share with everyone following information of drones as well space technologies like Satellites and record of Unidentified Aerial Phenomenon (U.A.P/U.F.O)". Personal attacks had led years of running along informing. An enemy found more at home then recognized with need of registry. Being all over the place and always of a need of lawyers to back them forward another day." Had the young Man made information of this public to his colleagues.

Central Intelligence Agency to the Secret Service still behind. All knew about these happenings and private ordeals yet wanted it quiet and living a life brainwashed by something otherworldly. They didn't care, perfect mastiffs bringing supplements to things that never even gave them their name. Preferring life with abusive mercenaries wasn't always the best case for a prisoner in his own home. Writing and capturing much of the monsters pursuing him and the precious people.

Meanwhile Video evidence and books of notes left in a locker only to be shared with a handful in closed doors. Yet spoke openly falsely on a dinner table of being part in saving the world.

Government snatching kids off the street for experiments and cravings left a headache of files. Dire of these events privately continuing in our cities regarded as "surveillance". Asking myself "Where is this going", "What if it updates getting further out of hand envelope everyone, endangering my family?"

There was only one answer to these events and it was to neutralize everything in our planets surroundings that sent a radio wave or other frequency. Problem was no one had prepared for this, being the biggest heart ache of it. It was obvious that if events did occur of things flying at you from somewhere else, *you ready and do the most direct of going out and prevailing the problem before it gets to you*. These observations had been hidden out of treason, thus the material consistently classified. Manipulated to harness, harness something no one in the mind knew how to control or what was being looked at, had there been real purpose.

The evidence was clear, these outer-space monsters being real. Something was having fun bumping in the night, playing deity and got tricked into complicating it. Sent it here from ancient slave labor of another planet stuck on making space ships/satellites their bloodlines kept as market. Market being space conquest and brain control as-well with mass manipulation in up keeping things their own methods. In a galactic scale dormant inside another flesh.

Government being needy got entangled with the military and everyone else around the world. Stabs the people in the back by mistake. Leaving brainwashed to forgive tyrants and murderers in the military. Broadcast privately everywhere of men, women and children's personal lives inside computers. Country under drone surveillance of stupendous White Supremacy in the modern world. Government hates to admit it, shoots everyone including themselves on the foot. It went on the comedy never ceased.

There was absolutely nothing brilliant of how these events set the world ablaze because of lunacy. Bleaching the world had been everything to these people, white washing the public with experimental space technologies and consistently disrupting domestic safety with it. Note that many of the nations problems had the root of evil coming from a team and their instruments only being involved in sales to survive.

Such as the satellites to clean the streets, It was their answer to escaping reality that anyone including themselves was a potential victim. Only proving those same selling the cure to human error of the day had been involved in spreading evil in the first place. While everyone else including China making their own shit show on the East with Russia. Living in a toxic bubble, dooms day clocks had already spun out of control.

It's how these space bugs wanted it. Running to them for answers and aid, chasing them right after telling them to leave, *hysterical.* Disgusting maggots of a fly seeing everything are these technologies. Salivating as saviors and the most obvious choice to rise from human evil. As if Human was always evil, they slaughtered their own people and committed humiliation.

Habits to point the finger at someone else was showing weakness and thus disfigured a image or solutions. *A child being breastfed had things inside its brain synchronized to drink out of a mothers breasts, the same older men were too caught.* Some wanted to market the child of a family and live inside a persons home as a solution for an afterlife. Working rigorously to body snatch and conscious theft of innocent.

Bastards destroyed everything and still asked us for physiological aid with balance. It just wouldn't work. I assure you it took years of work with very intelligent people to get this information out and it is always a damn good thing for everyone to know everything! It makes them Gods of their own you know!

Not to mention the "Hannibal Lector" routine they threw. Doing their job of criminal investigations, such a pity they had supervisors and heads of their department consistently played with strings. Initiative had just been sabotaged by the lazy and sophisticated mind controlled chairs of elected too. This was real, they left one guy to do his research and homework saving lives including his own.

While stunning his body technologically, disabling him with an alien precursor satellite system. It had the world shook, the question of who kept the guy alive while brutally dishonored had been too in the dark for years. Perhaps it was a addicts way of sexual misogamy and deep space entertainment. To watch many Innocent squirm over fear of prosecutions for the sins they've created and committed. It was no accident, they didn't go up the ladder.

Night had come again, similar setting from years ago.

Difference was there was no sound of cicadas or grasshoppers singing in the southern summer nights. Kid made a young man to a man. He was starting to mentor some of his work and findings already. Down fall was during the fight against now daily surveillance, he was being institutionalized in the dark. Everyone he'd speak to was also hacked by these systems with aid from his advisors from distant places limited of help with forced interests as the others in governments alerted.

They wanted to help him understand this complex existence in the world and all around. Such disaster, enemies of life, fiends had no code of ethnics or leadership to bestow proper direction to infantry in our military or political agenda for daily procedures. A battle of life or death was all around us. It was necessary to keep your mind up from drowning everyday. Military had gone rogue murdering the public and its innocence. Yet a chain of a snake biting its own tail was practical because of this market.

Targeting bodies daily with space psychotronic weaponry.

How lucky of certain other figures in the shadows flicking dangerous attacks away at a cost. Difficult times, certain elements in around kept a young man alive including his wit and the basic of meditation with a gift of entertainment at home. Media use such as Facebook other forms of public network sharing had too been very beneficial. Acquiring information from the stars had made him a target of everything.

Proper teams domestically following these investigations had finally broken out the curse looking for the monsters lurking. Only problem, on how led off some had been because their leaders brain altered in bed with these predators. They too absolutely knew what was going on. It was all bizarre of a routine, everyone knew how dangerous the Department of Defense and its branches operated and they we're being *its bitch*.

An appearance of a ferry off the coasts of Australia.

Intelligence agencies operating these vessels hid themselves in boats disguised in a manner to which the example of a "ferry" caught by the eye, in turn to be of reality being something else. Covered with cloaking instruments like a shroud. It was of foreign origin these tools and toys being abundant in their organizations. Australia soon to be proven itself just like NATO's familiar state of handling. Scavenging for ways to get out of trouble and so on, including hiding in very expensive boats.

Not just thee instruments being utilized it was also in a neutral bandwagon style play taking turns to talk out of trouble with the rest of an organizations banded interrogation habit. Many unfortunately left so corrupted being forced into the bad habit of helping a criminal involved in scheme. Haunting, when noticed how they could never break out the autocrats in these guilds of agencies, in which was more implemented in a high tech matrix.

Only a tip of evidence of what other capabilities they had was given of notice. Some of it was just very impressive.

Only thing about it, a handful of people not fit for daily luxury of life, as an opinion. Limited access to the trove of tech and information. *Secret Knowledge,* Is the magic in the computer that ran miracles. Keeping these things to themselves was old and makeshift of an idea. Medical, Psychological, Natural Healing, Romance, Luck, Persuasions, upgraded abilities, survival was in an ancient aliens server. When word would get out, it was of a strange protocol to stay to themselves. Abuse would follow from the idea of "using it" or "knowing it". Taking full advantage of Alien captivated attention directly in an individual's life, It was pleasurable to them to penetrate out of one another with people who knew nothing of what was eating out their heads.

Gorgeous Women left brainwashed to sleep with near Autistic Evil menace, the organ of a host being left near defective. Yet money was spent for these to engage as long as one another got a taste of pleasure. Nervous system hacking was normal to these people. Beings living inside your sex life and daily routines left a reminder. Us sold as deals, human memory or the soul in a semi conductor at wholesale being closed mouthed. Protected by those we trusted the most in the Country. It was important to progress the need for reality onto the world. **IT WOULD NOT BE KEPT IN THE DARK ANY LONGER.**

Children had been captive and never to bear sons or daughters of their own. Pretty little girls being touched underground for months while leaving them bone dry gave a smack on the face with the bible in hand. This is part of an expensive bad habit that outgrew the grace of the living. Videos would be passed like private ENTERTAINMENT in a computer, flash drive and floppy disk. With some taking the shit home, we had been developed to do the same. Our predecessors had been outmatched and dazed of what these being offered to the table when established communication came to be. Many sacrificed in vain to protect and shame this new found Eco-system. It was right to keep that idea of your own to debate.

Evidence they would call it. Instance of material such as would remain quiet. It wasn't the gift of wisdom and knowledge one would welcome. Yet it was lifting to know what man had and would face having the possibility to change the new day for existence.

-Independent musicians playing in the background it was time to catch some air.-

"Damn I need another bump", "Damn I need another Bump"! "You was one!, Now you less!, Cause you fuck'd with the

Best"!

"Damn I need another Bump, Damn I need another Bump"!

- Playa Misery

Best Secret Technique when facing such turmoils in life's endeavors had to be listening to music. It was of innocence that we being the only known species as mammal to copy a birds whistle. Free from things, as fundamental of a natural smile.

Everyday there was someone making music, a new song popping in was enough to take notice this interest as a way to taste, a life support and a way to calm the beasts acting against you. They'd soon be a shadow that could only follow, until the day action acted as energy stabilizing that freedom to close eyes and release from attachments. It was good.

Drinking plenty of fluids was an obvious means of detoxing from whatever food and foul things you'd consume through out the expanse in this voyage of finding articulacy in the small things. Kid was now a man having spent years under direct attacks from the unknown clinching its fists at the anger of resistance that was building up. Military had finally met its maker having left things so illusive from public ears and interests. **If a man of war and conquests was proven wise, they'd know better of acting at the instant.**

You need water to stay alive, its just the basic. If leadership was herding you through the desert, your civilization would be only punishing itself. Staying alive and having safer, balance means as cannasseur without disturbing your people was an evolutionary trait this age of space expanse, as a whole faced at dilemma. We needed to go manual and shoot what had been around us for so long eating and mating in our bodies..

Nurture of the cosmos was found to be present and flourishing. Big civilizations had introduced themselves with antidotes and medical genius. How unique for some to have found the answer for eternity in this dark expanse of matter while enduring weakness of loss. It had been of mastermind infusions to see these groups more than capable of anything thrown at them.

Galaxy teeming with life and everything was on a script. Science ruled all and reason was the pillars of life itself.

Reason had been attacked by space cultured rape for as long as time would be presenting of itself. Combination of aged tar with water would leave theory of life's basics from nothing. It was the secret of voyage in dark matters isotope element. An Elephant had all the answers and beat the shit out of a guy in front of everyone in the form of a cartoon. It really happened. Left him with a bag of money and a book the kid wrote himself and said good luck with everything. Showed him off to the neighbors and waved gracefully.

It indeed had been the need to push the efforts on space invader retaliation that had left itself to comfortable dormant in our minds. Our government had been malformed and tainted of its image, showing those in charge manipulated and unfit for our nations well balance. How these turn of events took place had been the result of being unprepared and unknowing of what potential threats we'd face together. It had been a secret war with the laws the universe played, where a selected young man had the challenge to understand reality around him. Our minds had been inside a computer for generations, it was time others to know.

Regarding the task at hand to have a scream echoed from the mouths of children would've proven the way to summon the devil with ease and catch him red handed. Question weather if God truly thrived in a machine had the spirit of itself been trapped. The kid had been myself locked in a room while everything crumbled, people around the world needed answers as to what was hurting them so much. Being in fact the oddity of perfect timing and flexing to impress genuine emotion was the reason to grow and age wiser.

Ultimate Evil was a very smart person that can change the world and everything around them. An extraordinary number of people worked hard to show someone of the right things and lessons of real mentorship. It's a damn shame so much pain had pummeled along the route. Being better had it been from blood of his blood and flesh of his flesh. Spirit had not been absent those years even to the wisest of Gods Creations, an atheist.

EN EL NOMBRE DEL PADRE, EL HIJO

Y EL ESPIRITU SANTO AMEN, Y AMEN.

GOD-SPEED

The theory was to stay parasitically attached to a "worthy" live host, whist traveling the stars in the future. For portions, years of ones personal life.

* Host from abduction.

Primitive technique to waste time in the stars.

Leeched to anothers skull.

Some of the best men & boys died
sitting down.

- Empty bottles (filled) once
  is all they could take.

- Dry without
  liquids to
  hydrate them.

- Shown   a
  young   boy
  in deep space
  traversal, likely
  the inside of an
  empty bottle,
  given to him
  since birth,
  a   canteen
  bottle of sorts.

  *Dying?

~There exists a tale
of a Precious Gem so massive &
Beautiful it was carried by a large
three headed being like our natural
"tortoise".

(Black, Red
Diamond)

~There are
ancient texts
found in a Black
market in space
that spoke of
these stories.

"At least
finish some
of our art."....

~To think
they had Miners

~Some of
these things
lived inside
us, connected
to brains cybernetically
Forcing Masturbation.

?

(son of a bitch) —They battle
this way for
distance. is
a problem for
them.

— (Grey , BLUE)

(More Advance)
(Monsterous)

Messages

— Signals travel —
Light years —

"It JUST
WANTS
TO KISS!"
Kill the
Kid !!!

ALRH CENTARU

Computer

— Grey Hybrid

"We're millions of years old."

Our concious, brain & body...replicated!

We we're "changed" too.
     (monkeys)

"Maman, mejor te mato.!!"

"Do you know theres giants
who bask in nothing!"

— It was
a study you
could see...

— Some are giants

THE STORY OF KITE, STOLEN THE
SACRED EGG OF KNOWLEDGE, FROM PRIMORDIAL!